the genocide reader

the politics of ethnicity and extermination

IDEAS in CONFLICT

Marnie J. McCuen

GARY McCUEN
publications inc.

411 Mallalieu Drive
Hudson, Wisconsin 54016
Phone (715) 386-7113

JC
328.6
.G 360
2000

Illustrations and Photo Credits

John Jonik 66; Kitty Kennedy 30; 41; 137; Eleanor Mill 158; Joel Pett 163; Steve Sack 82; 120; Richard Wright 145.

GARY McCUEN publications inc.

© 2000 by Gary E. McCuen Publications, Inc.
411 Mallalieu Drive, Hudson, Wisconsin 54016

(715) 386-7113

International Standard Book Number
0-86596-184-0
Printed in the United States of America

CONTENTS

Ideas in Conflict

Chapter 3   **CAMBODIA'S KILLING FIELDS: THE U.S., THE KHMER ROUGE AND GENOCIDE**

Chapter 4 NEVER AGAIN? COMMITMENT TO STOP RWANDAN GENOCIDE

REASONING SKILL DEVELOPMENT

These activities may be used as individualized study guides for students in libraries and resource centers or as discussion catalysts in small group and classroom discussions.

IDEAS
in C🌐NFLICT

This series features ideas in conflict on political, social, and moral issues. It presents counterpoints, debates, opinions, commentary, and analysis for use in libraries and classrooms. Each title in the series uses one or more of the following basic elements:

Introductions that present an issue overview giving historic background and/or a description of the controversy.

Counterpoints and debates carefully chosen from publications, books, and position papers on the political right and left to help librarians and teachers respond to requests that treatment of public issues be fair and balanced.

Symposiums and forums that go beyond debates that can polarize and oversimplify. These present commentary from across the political spectrum that reflect how complex issues attract many shades of opinion.

A *global* emphasis with foreign perspectives and surveys on various moral questions and political issues that will help readers to place subject matter in a less culture-bound and ethnocentric frame of reference. In an ever-shrinking and interdependent world, understanding and cooperation are essential. Many issues are global in nature and can be effectively dealt with only by common efforts and international understanding.

Reasoning skill study guides and discussion activities provide ready-made tools for helping with critical reading and evaluation of content. The guides and activities deal with one or more of the following:

RECOGNIZING AUTHOR'S POINT OF VIEW

INTERPRETING EDITORIAL CARTOONS

VALUES IN CONFLICT

WHAT IS EDITORIAL BIAS?

WHAT IS SEX BIAS?

WHAT IS POLITICAL BIAS?

WHAT IS ETHNOCENTRIC BIAS?

WHAT IS RACE BIAS?

WHAT IS RELIGIOUS BIAS?

*From across **the political spectrum** varied sources are presented for research projects and classroom discussions. Diverse opinions in the series come from magazines, newspapers, syndicated columnists, books, political speeches, foreign nations, and position papers by corporations and nonprofit institutions.*

About the Publisher

The late Gary E. McCuen was an editor and publisher of anthologies for libraries and discussion materials for schools and colleges. His publications have specialized in social, moral and political conflict. They include books, pamphlets, cassettes, tabloids, filmstrips and simulation games, most of them created from his many years of experience in teaching and educational publishing.

READING

1

CONTEMPORARY UNDER-STANDING OF GENOCIDE:
CONCEPTS AND QUESTIONS

Peter J. Stoett

Peter J. Stoett is a Professor of Political Science. This essay was awarded the Marvin Gelber Prize for 1994. Established in recognition of the abiding interest of Marvin Gelber in international affairs and his many years of service to the Canadian Institute of International Affairs (CIIA), the prize is awarded annually for an article by a junior Canadian scholar.

■ **POINTS TO CONSIDER**

1. Discuss the importance of defining the term "genocide." Summarize Stoett's examples of the term "genocide" used for "political purposes."

2. Who is Raphael Lemkin?

3. Explain the importance of the Nazi Holocaust in a modern understanding of genocide.

4. Describe the minimalist and maximalist definitions of genocide. What are the strengths and limitation of both?

5. What roles do the individual, the sovereign nation-state and the international community play in the perpetuation and prevention of genocide?

Excerpted from Peter J. Stoett, "This Age of Genocide: Conceptual and Institutional Implications," **International Journal,** vol. 50, no. 3 (summer 1995), published by the Canadian Institute of International Affairs (CIAA). Reprinted with permission, CIIA.

The best way to ensure that sovereign states do not resort to genocide is to promote their inclusion in a universal, but necessarily limited, human rights agenda.

...There is much in a word, especially one as connotative as *genocide,* which from any standpoint involves death and human suffering. It has immediate and public policy implications, as the Rwandan case demonstrates: according to one report, late in May 1994, when the killings had reached a frenzied peak and over 500,000 Tutsis and moderate Hutus had probably been massacred, the "U.S. Government had instructed its spokesmen not to label the deaths in Rwanda 'genocide,' since doing so would have made it more difficult to stand aside and watch the slaughter continue."[1] Of course, the word isn't always hidden from public view; it can be used for specific political purposes as well. For example, the Reagan Administration called the evacuation of villages on the upper Coco River in Nicaragua by the Sandinista government "genocide." Though the resettlement was indeed forced and involved the abuse of an indigenous population (the Miskito Indians), it was not the mass slaughter usually associated with the word.[2] However, this example is an exception: the word seems to be a psychological barrier, which once passed demands increased attention. Genocide is usually recognized as the ultimate crime against humanity; yet its definition remains contested.

DEFINING GENOCIDE: A MINIMALIST DEFINITION

The word *genocide* was coined by Polish jurist Raphael Lemkin during the implementation of Hitler's Final Solution. Lemkin was aware of the atrocities being waged across Europe, largely on racial grounds and affecting one ethnic group in particular: European Jews. Thus he introduced a new term "to denote an old practice in its modern development," derived from the Greek word for race or people, *genos,* and the Latin *caedere* or *cide,* to kill.[3] A word born from the Holocaust has grown as a concept with the passage of time and the persistence of atrocity....

The minimalist definition has its basis in the Convention on the Prevention and Punishment of the Crime of Genocide, which grew out of worldwide condemnation of the Nazi Holocaust (1939-45). Some argue that the word should be reserved solely for that historical event, though this is an increasingly rare position.[4] *Genocide* was first used at the United Nations in General

Assembly resolution 96 (I) of 11 December 1946. It is interesting to note that the United Nations secretariat had originally drafted a Convention which "subsumed under *genocide* such acts as destroying the specific characteristics of groups by destroying their shrines, the confiscation of their property, the deprivation of their means of livelihood, the prohibition of their language, [and] the destruction of their books."[5]

In the end, a narrower definition was accepted and remains standing today....

The Convention makes clear that genocide is a crime in times of peace as well as war and that a state's actions towards its own citizens could be considered a breach of international law. Genocide may also be committed against people in states other than the one most concerned — an implication not only that states will be the prime perpetrators but that certain war crimes committed under occupation may be viewed as genocide. The following acts are also punishable: conspiracy to commit genocide, direct and public incitement to commit genocide, attempts to commit genocide, and complicity in genocide (no doubt a reference to Holocaust collaborators in occupied states during the War).[6]...

The Convention's explicit emphasis on ethnic identity and groups is understandable in light of the centrality of the doctrine of racial superiority in Nazi ideology. But in practice it is often cited as a limitation. For example, when the Khmer Rouge killed well over one million Cambodians, Pol Pot could not be charged with genocide because he was not targeting a specific ethnic or racial group....

CRIMES OF THE NATION-STATE

Though the Convention clearly makes it possible to charge individuals, including non-state actors, with genocide, one thing is fairly certain: the cold logistics of genocide suggest the presence of the state — although politics prevent the Convention from articulating this — since few other organized groups could have the apparatus necessary to carry out the crime; and since governments have leaders, regardless of their particular hierarchy, those at the top must be the chief criminals. The Nuremberg trials were quite explicit in establishing the precedent that "following orders" is an insufficient defense against a charge of crimes against humanity: individuals must be held accountable. Yet — and here we begin to move away from a narrow criminal definition of genocide — sociological theory has challenged the conventional notion that the intent of individual murderers is the sole cause of genocide. Helen Fein believes that genocide is "organized state murder."[7] Wulf Kansteiner explores the current transformation in the "representation of Nazism from an exceptional to an exemplary historical period."[8]...

A MAXIMALIST DEFINITION

The advent of the nuclear age takes us further toward an alternative and expanded perspective on genocide. It can be argued that nuclear deterrence with its threat of mass annihilation was the ultimate genocidal policy. Of course, it can also be argued that the threat of nuclear war introduced a new concept into the lexicon, that of *omnicide.* However, since nuclear strategy was predicated upon the destruction of a specific enemy, omnicide was not contemplated (though it did not take a particularly bright individual to predict that it would result). It is this element of intention, or even incitement, that has led some to call the nuclear arms race genocidal....

Such concerns move us toward the "maximalist" conception of genocide. The state remains pivotal: in many cases, what is often called "state terrorism" (coercive violence perpetrated by states against their own or other citizens) is seen as genocide. Murder takes many forms, including state murder. The deliberate starvation of entire communities, and the use of food as a weapon in general; the lack of clean water in the slums of major cities; the destruction of East Timor by the Indonesian military, or of Tibet by the Chinese, or of parts of Indochina by the Americans, or of political opponents of various Soviet regimes; or the drainage of marshes in southern Iraq: all involve mass death, inflicted with obvious intent. By such an expanded definition, war is genocide. Cultural destruction that has a physical component, commonly called *ethnocide,* is a type of genocide; so is the construction of large-scale dams that displace millions of people, Himalayan deforestation that causes floods, and other forms of *ecocide.* The list cannot end here. Female *infanticide* in countries like India and China may be viewed as a form of genocide over time. The reluctance of some Asian and African governments to respond to the health needs of AIDS patients could be viewed as genocidal. Noam Chomsky refers to American coercive trading in the tobacco sector as the "blurring of the boundary between narco-trafficking and genocide."[9] An estimated eleven million children die each year from easily preventable diseases such as measles, pneumonia, and diarrhea. Hiroshi Nakajima, the director-general of the World Health Organization, has called them victims of "silent genocide." Similarly, Henry Shue writes of the "Holocaust of neglect."[10]

COLONIZATION

Likewise it could be claimed that the colonization of the "New World," a process called imperialism by some and progress by others, was a genocidal process which continues today. This leads to interesting alternative interpretations of the Convention and of state responsibility. For example, in October 1992 an International Tribunal of Indigenous Peoples and Oppressed Nations in the United States unanimously found the United States government guilty of numerous violations of international law, including the 1948 Genocide Convention.[11] More broadly, the modern nation-state, which demands a certain level of assimilation, could be seen as a genocidal machine. As one commentator suggested, "the fiction of the nation-state is seldom innocuous. It often contains a prescription for the cultural destruction of a people through state policies of more or less compulsory assimilation and, at the limit, for genocide."[12] By extension, then, the state-system that supports the nation-state as the primary political unit could be seen as a genocidal accomplice. Leo Kuper, on the related principle of non-intervention, writes that "the sovereign territorial state claims, as an integral part of its sovereignty, the right to commit genocide...and the United Nations, for all practical purposes, defends this right."[13] If the state is the heart of the problem, any talk of humane intervention is tinged with irony, perhaps even hypocrisy.

BLURRING THE LINES?

The list of possible instances (and culprits) of genocide, then, appears endless. This is precisely the problem, minimalists would argue: a maximalist approach blurs the lines among genocide, aggression, violence, suffering, and other bad things. Alain Destexhe insists that "there is a difference between a civilian killed in an air raid or from cholera in a refugee camp and one deliberately chosen for death on the grounds of being born a Jew or a Tutsi." For him, only the Armenian massacre by the Young Turks of the Ottoman Empire (1915-16), the Holocaust, and the recent Rwandan carnage qualify as true genocide.[14] This might be an extreme position, but the minimalists do have a point. The

12

problem with relating the maximalist definition to the Convention is that the latter includes the problematic terms "deliberately" and "calculated," which means that in the case of high child mortality in the South or inner-city gun-slayings in the North, one must assume a planned policy by others, specifically the oppressors. This is a positivist element in the identification of the criminal that clashes with sociological models of systematic infliction of suffering or structural violence....

SOVEREIGNTY AS DETERRENT

The creation of states can be seen as a deterrent to genocide and as a promotion of ethnic rights. For example, the "perceived need for Armenians and Jews to have respective territories...to prevent future genocide is an obvious example of the reaction of a community which fears for its survival."[15] In this light sovereignty is protective. Simultaneously, the legal implications of sovereignty and its connection to the ruling élites of states mean protection of another kind: freedom from external intervention in the affairs of states which may well be inciting and committing genocide at this very moment. As usual in world politics, the double-edged sword is very sharp....

Sovereignty affects the minimalist conception of genocide since, [it] remains pivotal, manifested in (selective) adherence to the principle of non-intervention; as Kuper insists, states play the main role in genocidal activities, and the institution of sovereignty perpetuates the modern nation-state. However, the idea that national sovereignty is solely responsible for the possibility of genocide is supportable only if it can be cogently argued that its absence would result in a world free from genocide....

Sovereignty affects the maximalist definition as well, since any attempt to deal with social injustice must involve nation-states or, to be more precise, governments. This is not to reduce the importance of the role played by non-governmental organizations (NGOs) and, better, community-based development initiatives. However, governments are the only organizations capable of dealing with modern humanitarian emergencies, and thus the development of institutions which engage multilateral responses is vital. At the same time, there is little doubt that once an extraordinarily oppressive regime is recognized as a sovereign entity, the chances of modifying its behavior by rhetorical condemnation are reduced. (In an age of economic globalization, regimes like

Myanmar's State Law and Order Restoration Council continue to attract foreign capital.) And it is even less likely that the dominant powers will receive or consider such condemnation themselves. How would Canadian officials respond to charges that Canada is an apartheid state, that the high suicide rate among northern aboriginals constitutes a form of genocide? Again, the ambiguity of the maximalist position limits its utility.

JUSTICE

With regard to justice, the minimalist focus is on punitive measures to enforce or promote the Convention. The persistence of sovereignty has made the pursuit of legal justice almost impossible, since the very perpetrators of the crime (states) are in essence immune from prosecution (though some individuals may eventually be punished during or after transition stages). The maximalist position, on the other hand, is closer to an entitlement orientation. This is the place for the broader questions of North-South, or even more generally rich-poor, relations....

Of course, some people, less sanguine about the human prospect than liberal institutionalists, suggest that sovereignty and contemporary perspectives on justice are ephemeral. An immutable human nature leads inexorably to conflict and often violence; even, perhaps, to the gates of Auschwitz. This fatalistic vision is best left for debate amongst philosophers and theologians. It is enough to say here that violence in any form is the result of moral relaxation, and that power and paranoia make a bad mix.

THE UNITED NATIONS

What then of the United Nations, the primary institution in world affairs? While the overwhelming endorsement of the Convention on the Prevention and Punishment of the Crime of Genocide is heartening, putting even a dull set of teeth in the Convention is another story. Barbara Harff believes that we need "a re-cognition of the essential juridical truth that genocide transcends the interests of states and individuals. In other words, if genocide is a crime under international law, as all agree, then it is everyone's responsibility to impress upon policy makers the necessity to act upon violations of it."[16] The scheduled tribunals charged with bringing war criminals from the Yugoslavian [Bosnian] conflict to justice may be a start. Though the

International Law Commission is working on a related treaty, it remains to be seen if Bosnia or Rwanda can provide sufficient impetus for the creation of a permanent criminal tribunal with general jurisdiction.[17]

Draft statutes for a permanent court to try cases of genocide, war crimes, terrorism, and drug trafficking exist. But what court could realistically deal with the Rwandan case? Rwanda's new prime minister, Faustin Twagiramungu, has stated that no less than 22,000 employees of the former government are suspected of complicity in the slayings that gripped the country in the spring of 1994, thousands more were part of the killing militia known as the "Interahamwe," and thousands of Hutu citizens killed Tutsi neighbours and participated in mob killings — all this in a country with but a skeleton of its own court system intact. While some top officials may be tried — only because the former government lost a war (it will be a more difficult feat in the former Yugoslavia) — it is simply unrealistic to assume all those involved in murder will be charged. What about all the Chetniks who participated in the genocidal rape campaign in Bosnia? The same will probably hold true for the trials to take place in Ethiopia for crimes committed under Mengistu Haile Mariam's brutal rule. The 1979 "trial" and execution of the self-declared president-for-life, Francisco Macias Nguema, hardly resolved things in Equatorial Guinea. Justice cannot be complete in such matters, and it will often be used to establish the moral legitimacy of a new élite. The United Nations, despite its internationalist ethos, cannot avoid the charge that it is simply aiding this process....

INTERNATIONAL INTERVENTION FORCE

The argument that the United Nations should become active in fighting civil wars is much less convincing.[18] Most civil wars involving genocide would force the United Nations to fight directly against governments and on the side of rebels, an unlikely scenario given the reluctance of member-states to support such campaigns. Indeed, the opposite is possible: the United Nations could end up preserving "order" even when civil rebellion is justified. There is no disinterested omniscient force to determine the validity of such intervention at the political level.

Another consideration is that in any modern intervention, great losses can be expected. How, then, can the United Nations attract the personnel necessary for humanitarian relief (assuming it does not resort to hiring mercenaries)? Over time, the United Nations cannot police such situations, a frustrating fact and one that the fashionable zeal for rapid intervention obscures. From a foreign policy perspective, the cold, hard reality for decision-makers is that armed intervention to stop genocide will demand public acceptance of the potential loss of life....

Since some schemes for United Nations reform would create an armed force at the disposal of the secretary-general, does it make moral sense for the office which heads an institution established for the purpose of conflict resolution to give orders to engage in armed conflict?...

CONVERGING PERSPECTIVES

Finally, we might argue with those whom Mark Zacher and Richard Matthews call Republican Liberals[19] that if the spread of democracy and the rule of law can help avoid international warfare, perhaps it can also reduce the use of genocide as state policy. Some adherents of the maximalist position would reject this out of hand, since liberal democracies are implicit culprits in the suffering of the masses. But the minimalist perspective would be much more friendly, since whatever openness in government there might be would surely reduce the likelihood that such a government would commit genocide as defined in the Convention. Here the two perspectives might even converge: the best way to ensure that sovereign states do not resort to genocide is to promote their inclusion in a universal, but necessarily limited, human rights agenda....

NOTES FOR READING ONE

[1] Milton Leitenberg, "Anatomy of a Massacre," *New York Times,* 31 July 1994, 15.

[2] See Hurst Hannum, *Autonomy, Sovereignty, and Self-Determination: the Accommodation of Conflicting Rights* (Philadelphia: University of Pennsylvania Press 1990), 220.

[3] See his landmark *Axis Rule in Occupied Europe* (Washington DC: Carnegie Endowment 1944), 79.

[4] During the 1970 Senate Foreign Relations Sub-Committee Hearings on the Genocide Convention and Its Aftermath, the committee chair, Senator Frank Church, wondered aloud if the Convention wasn't 'really an effort to pound a few more nails into Hitler's coffin' (United States Senate, Hearings Before a Subcommittee of the Committee on Foreign Relations, 91st cong, 2nd sess, 1970. 61-2). Because of concern over the convention's implications for sovereignty and federalism, the Senate rejected ratification until 1986.

16

[5] Nagendra Singh, "The Development of International Law," in Adam Roberts and Benedict Kingsbury, eds, *United Nations, Divided World: The UN's Roles in International Relations* (Oxford: Clarendon Press 1993), 394. The Draft Convention is UN doc. E/447 (1947).

[6] Article III, Convention on the Prevention and Punishment of the Crime of Genocide, adopted unanimously by the United Nations General Assembly, 9 December 1948; *United Nations Treaty Series 78* (1948), 277. Entered into force 12 January 1951.

[7] Helen Fein, *Accounting for Genocide: National Response and Jewish Victimization During the Holocaust* (New York: Free Press 1979), 7.

[8] Wulf Kansteiner, "From Exception to Exemplum: the New Approach to Nazism and the 'Final Solution'." *History and Theory: Studies in the Philosophy of History* 33 (no 2, 1994), 145-71, 147.

[9] Noam Chomsky, *Deterring Democracy* (New York & London: Verso, 1991), 127. Chomsky compares current American policies with the Opium War (1839-42).

[10] Hiroshi Nakajima quoted in Chomsky, *ibid,* 241; for Shue, see his *Basic Rights: Subsistence, Affluence, and U.S. Foreign Policy* (Princeton NJ: Princeton University Press 1980).

[11] *Verdict of the International Tribunal of Indigenous Peoples and Oppressed Nations in the USA* (San Francisco: American Indian Movement, 4 October 1992). Reported in the Internet on the Holocaust and Genocide, 44-46, 1993, 13-14.

[12] Pierre van den Berghe, "Introduction," in van den Berghe, ed, *State Violence and Ethnicity* (Niwot CO: University Press of Colorado 1990), 6.

[13] Leo Kuper, *Genocide* (New Haven CT: Yale University Press 1981), 161. Note, however, that he assumes a minimalist definition of genocide in his work.

[14] Alain Destexhe, "The Third Genocide," *Foreign Policy* 97 (winter 1994-5), 4.

[15] Hannum, *Autonomy, Sovereignty, and Self-Determination,* 464.

[16] Barbara Harff, *Genocide and Human Rights: International Legal and Political Issues,* Monograph Series in World Affairs, 20:3 (Denver CO: Graduate School of International Studies, University of Denver, 1985), 68. See also her *Genocide and Human Rights: International Legal and Political Issues* (Denver: University of Denver Press 1984).

[17] See Theodor Meron, "The Case for War Crimes Trials in Yugoslavia," *Foreign Affairs* 72 (summer 1993), 122-35.

[18] For contrasting perspectives, see H. Scott Fairley, "State Actors, Humanitarian Intervention and International Law: Reopening the Pandora's Box," *Georgia Journal of International and Cooperative Law* 10 (no 1, 1980), 29-63; and Thomas Weiss and Larry Minear, "Do International Ethics Matter? Humanitarian Politics and the Sudan," *Ethics and International Affairs* 5 (1991), 197-214. More generally, see R.J. Vincent's challenging *Nonintervention and International Order* (Princeton: Princeton University Press 1974).

[19] Mark Zacher and Richard Matthews, "Liberal International Theory: Common Threads, Divergent Strands," in Charles Kegley, ed, *Controversies in International Relations Theory: Realism and the Neoliberal Challenge* (New York: St. Martin's 1995), 122-3.

CHAPTER 1

DEFINING GENOCIDE: THE DESTRUCTION OF EUROPEAN JEWS

GENOCIDE: A MODERN CRIME, GLOBAL CONSEQUENCES

Raphael Lemkin

Raphael Lemkin, the creator of the term genocide, *was born June 24, 1901, near Bezwodene, Poland. He began a law career as a public prosecutor for the District Court of Poland. In 1933, Lemkin submitted a proposal to the League of Nations arguing for the criminalization under international law, of destruction of any racial, social or religious group. The proposal was not adopted. Lemkin continued his law career in private practice in Warsaw. In 1939, Germany invaded Poland. Lemkin fought with the guerrilla resistance, then in 1940, fled to Sweden. He was one of two members of his family (of over 40 members) to survive the War. After the War, with full light upon the atrocities the Germans committed against the Jews and other civilian populations, Lemkin continued his crusade to have genocide made a crime under international law.*

■ POINTS TO CONSIDER

1. Why does the author coin the term *genocide?*
2. Summarize Lemkin's definition of genocide.
3. Describe the National Socialists' means to gain favor of the German people for genocidal policies.
4. List the components of genocidal technique which Lemkin describes. Discuss two in detail.
5. Assess Lemkin's argument for treating genocide as a crime under international law.
6. Who was affected by Germany's genocidal policies, according to Lemkin?

Excerpted from an article by Raphael Lemkin submitted for the U.S. House of Representatives Committee on Foreign Affairs, 22 March 1945.

Germany has transformed an ancient barbarity into a principle of government by dignifying genocide as a sacred purpose of the German people.

"One of the great mistakes of 1918 was to spare the civil life of the enemy countries, for it is necessary for us Germans to be always at least double the numbers of the peoples of the contiguous countries. We are therefore obliged to destroy at least a third of their inhabitants. The only means is organized underfeeding, which in this case is better than machine guns."

The speaker was Marshal von Rundstedt addressing the Reich War Academy in Berlin in 1943. He was only aping the Fuehrer, who had said, "Natural instincts bid all living human beings not merely conquer their enemies but also destroy them." In former days it was the victor's prerogative to destroy tribes, entire peoples.

OLD PRACTICE, MODERN UNDERSTANDING

Hitler was right. The crime of the Reich in wantonly and deliberately wiping out whole peoples is not utterly new in the world. It is only new in the civilized world as we have come to think of it. It is so new in the traditions of civilized man that he has no name for it.

It is for this reason that I took the liberty of inventing the word "genocide." The term is from the Greek word *genos* meaning tribe or race and the Latin *cide* meaning killing. Genocide tragically enough must take its place in the dictionary of the future beside other tragic words like "homicide" and "infanticide." As Von Rundstedt has suggested the term does not necessarily signify mass killings, although it may mean that. More often it refers to a coordinated plan aimed at destruction of the essential foundation of the life of national groups so that these groups wither and die like plants that have suffered a blight. The end may be accomplished by the forced disintegration of political and social institutions, of the culture of the people, of their language, their national feelings, and their religion. It may be accomplished by wiping out all bases of personal security, liberty, health, and dignity. When these means fail the machine gun can always be utilized as a last resort. Genocide is directed against a national group as an entity, and the attack on individuals is only secondary to the annihilation of the national group to which they belong.

20

Such terms as "denationalization" or "Germanization" which have been used till now do not adequately convey the full force of the new phenomenon of genocide. They signify only the substitution of the national pattern of the oppressor for the original national pattern but not the destruction of the biological and physical structure of the oppressed group.

PHILOSOPHY OF GENOCIDE

Germany has transformed an ancient barbarity into a principle of government by dignifying genocide as a sacred purpose of the German people. National Socialism is the doctrine of the biological superiority of the German people. Long before the War Nazi leaders were unblushingly announcing to the world and propagandizing to the Germans themselves the program of genocide they had elaborated. Like Hitler and Von Rundstedt, the official Nazi philosopher, Alfred Rosenberg, declared: "History and the mission of the future no longer mean the struggle of class against class, the struggle of church dogma against dogma, but the clash between blood and blood, race and race, people and people." As the German war machine placed more and more defeated nations under the full control of Nazi authorities, their civilian populations found themselves exposed to the bloodthirsty and methodical application of the German program of genocide.

A hierarchy of racial values determined the ultimate fate of the many peoples that fell under German domination. Jews were to be completely annihilated. The Poles, the Slovenes, the Czechs, the Russians, and all other inferior Slav peoples were to be kept on the lowest social levels. Those felt to be related by blood, the Dutch, the Norwegian, the Alsatians, etc., were to have the alternatives of entering the German community by espousing "Germanism" or of sharing the fate of the inferior peoples.

TECHNIQUES OF GENOCIDE

All aspects of nationhood were exposed to the attacks of the genocidal policy.

Political—The political cohesion of the conquered countries was intended to be weakened by dividing them into more or less self-contained and hermetically enclosed zones, as in the four zones of France, the ten zones of Yugoslavia, the five zones of Greece; by partitioning their territories to create puppet states, like

21

Croatia and Slovakia; by detaching territory for incorporation in the Greater Reich, as was done with western Poland, Alsace-Lorraine, Luxembourg, Slovenia. Artificial boundaries were created to prevent communication and mutual assistance by the national groups involved.

In the incorporated areas of western Poland, Luxembourg, Alsace-Lorraine, Eupen, Malmedy, Moresnet, local administrations were replaced by German administrative organization. The legal system was recast on the German model. Special commissioners for the strengthening of Germanism, attached to each administration, coordinated the activities designed to foster and promote Germanism. They were assisted by local inhabitants of German origin. These, duly registered and accredited, served as a nucleus of Germanism and enjoyed special privileges with respect to food rations, employment, and position.

National allegiances were impaired by creating puppet governments, as in Greece, Norway, and France, and by supporting national Nazi parties. Where the people, such as the Poles, could not achieve the dignity of embracing Germanism, they were expelled from the area and their territory (western Poland) was to be Germanized by colonization.

Social—The social structure of a nation is vital to its national development. Therefore the German occupants endeavored to bring about changes that weakened national spiritual resources. The focal point of this attack has been the intelligentsia, because this group largely provides leadership. In Poland and Slovenia the intellectuals and the clergy were, to a large extent, either murdered or removed for forced labor in Germany. Intellectuals and resistants of all occupied countries were marked for execution. Even among the blood-related Dutch some 23,000 were killed, the greater number of them being leading members of their communities.

Cultural—The Germans sought to obliterate every reminder of former cultural patterns. In the incorporated areas the local language, place names, personal names, public signs, and inscriptions were supplanted by German equivalents. German was to be the language of the courts, of the schools, of the government, and of the street. In Alsace-Lorraine and Luxembourg, French was not even permitted as a language to be studied in primary schools. The function of the schools was to preserve and strengthen Naziism. Attendance at a German school was compulsory through the

22

primary grades and three years of secondary school.

In Poland, although Poles could receive vocational training, they were denied any liberal arts training, since that might stimulate independent national thinking. To prohibit artistic expression of a national culture, rigid controls were established. Not only were the radio, the press, and the cinema closely supervised, but every painter, musician, architect, sculptor, writer, actor, and theatrical producer required a license to continue his artistic activities.

Religious—Wherever religion represented a vital influence in the national life, the spiritual power of the church was undermined by various means. In Luxembourg children over 14 were protected by law against criticism if they should renounce their religious affiliations for membership in Nazi youth organizations. In the puppet state of Croatia an independent but German-dominated Orthodox Church was created for Serbs, in order to destroy forever the spiritual ties with the Patriarch at Belgrade. With the special violence and thoroughness reserved for Poles and Jews, Polish church property was pillaged and despoiled and the clergy subjected to constant persecution.

Moral—Hand in hand with the undermining of religious influence went devices for the moral debasement of national groups. Pornographic publications and movies were foisted upon the Poles. Alcohol was kept cheap although food became increasingly dear, and peasants were legally bound to accept spirits for agricultural produce. Although under Polish law gambling houses had been prohibited, German authorities not only permitted them to come into existence, but relaxed the otherwise severe curfew law.

Economic—The genocidal purpose of destroying or degrading the economic foundations of national groups was to lower the standard of living and to sharpen the struggle for existence, that no energies might remain for a cultural or national life. Jews were immediately deprived of the elemental means of existence, by expropriation and by forbidding them the right to work. Polish property in western incorporated Poland was confiscated and Poles denied licenses to practice trades or handicrafts, thus reserving trade for the Germans. The post office savings bank in western Poland taken over by the occupying authorities, assured the financial superiority of Germans by repaying deposits only to certificated Germans. In Slovenia the financial cooperatives and agricultural associations were liquidated. Among the blood-related peoples (Luxembourgers, Alsatians) the acceptance of Germanism was the criterion by which participation in the economic life was determined.

Biological—The genocidal policy was far-sighted as well as immediate in its objectives. On the one hand an increase in the birth rate, legitimate or illegitimate, was encouraged within Germany and among *Volksdeutsche* in the occupied countries. Subsidies were offered for children begotten by Germany military men by women of related blood such as Dutch and Norwegian. On the other hand, every means to decrease the birth rate among racial inferiors was used. Millions of war prisoners and forced laborers from all the conquered countries of Europe were kept from contact with their wives. Poles in incorporated Poland met obstacles in trying to marry among themselves. Chronic under-nourishment, deliberately created by the occupant, tended not only to discourage the birth rate but also to increase infant mortality. Coming generations in Europe were thus planned to be predominantly of German blood, capable of overwhelming all other races by sheer numbers.

Physical—The most direct and drastic of the techniques of genocide is simply murder. It may be the slow and scientific murder by mass starvation or the swift but no less scientific murder by mass extermination in gas chambers, wholesale executions or exposure to disease and exhaustion. Food rationing in all territory under German domination was established on racial principles, ranging in 1943 from 93 percent of its pre-war diet for the German inhabitants to 20 percent of its pre-war diet for the Jewish population. A carefully graduated scale allowed protein rations of 97 percent to the Germans, 95 percent to the Dutch, 71 percent to the French, 38 percent to the Greeks, and 20 percent to the Jews. For fats, where there was the greatest shortage, the rations were 77 percent to the Germans, 65 percent to the Dutch, 40 percent to the French, and 0.32 percent to the Jews.

Specific vitamin deficiencies were created on a scientific basis.

The rise in the death rate among the various groups reflects this feeding program. The death rate in the Netherlands was ten per thousand; Belgium, 14 per thousand; Bohemia and Moravia, 13.4 per thousand. The mortality in Warsaw was 2,160 Aryans in September 1941, as compared to 800 in September 1938, and for the Jews in Warsaw, 7,000 in September 1941, as against 306 in September 1938.

Such elementary necessities of life as warm clothing, blankets, and firewood in winter were either withheld or requisitioned from Poles and Jews. Beginning with the winter of 1940-41 the Jews in the Warsaw ghetto received no fuel at all. Even God's clean air was denied — the Jews in the overcrowded ghettos were forbidden the use of public parks. The authoritative report of the War Refugee Board published in November 1944, and the overwhelming new evidence that appears daily of the brutal mass killings that have taken place in such notorious death camps as Majdanek and Oswiecim [Auschwitz] are sufficient indication of the scope of the German program.

In Birkenau alone between April 1942 and April 1944 approximately 1,765,000 Jews were gassed. Some 5,600,000 Jews and around 2,000,000 Poles have been murdered or died as a result of the extermination policies. Whole communities have been exterminated. It is estimated, for instance, that of the 140,000 Dutch Jews who lived in the Netherlands before Occupation, only some 7,000 now survive, the rest being transferred to Poland for slaughter.

INTERNATIONAL IMPLICATIONS

Why should genocide be recognized as an international problem? Why not treat it as an internal problem of every country, if committed in time of peace, or as a problem between belligerents, if committed in time of war?

The practices of genocide anywhere affect the vital interests of all civilized people. Its consequences can neither be isolated nor localized. Tolerating genocide is an admission of the principle that one national group has the right to attack another because of its supposed racial superiority. This principle invites an expansion of such practices beyond the borders of the offending state, and that means wars of aggression.

The disease of criminality, if left unchecked, is contagious. Minorities of one sort or another exist in all countries, protected by the constitutional order of the state. If persecution of any minority by any country is tolerated anywhere, the very moral and legal foundations of constitutional government may be shaken.

International trade depends upon confidence in the ability of individuals participating in the interchange of goods to fulfill their obligations. Arbitrary and wholesale confiscations of the properties and economic rights of whole groups of citizens of one state deprives them of the possibilities of discharging their obligations to citizens of other states, who thereby are penalized.

A source of international friction is created by unilateral withdrawal of citizen rights and even by expulsion of whole minority groups to other countries. The expulsions of law-abiding residents from Germany before this War has created friction with the neighboring countries to which these people were expelled. Moreover mass persecutions force mass flight. Thus the normal migration between countries assumes pathological dimensions.

Our whole cultural heritage is a product of the contributions of all peoples. We can best understand this when we realize how impoverished our culture would be if the so-called inferior peoples doomed by Germany, such as the Jews, had not been permitted to create the Bible or to give birth to an Einstein, a Spinoza; if the Poles had not had the opportunity to give to the world a Copernicus, a Chopin, a Curie; the Czechs a Huss and a Dvorak; the Greeks a Plato and a Socrates; the Russians, a Tolstoy and a Shostakovich.

SAFEGUARDS AND REMEDIES

The significance of a policy of genocide to the world order and to human culture is so great as to make it imperative that a system of safeguards be devised. The principle of the international protection of minorities was proclaimed by post-Versailles minority treaties. These treaties, however, were inadequate because they were limited to a few newly created countries. They were established mainly with the aim of protecting political and civil rights, rather than the biological structure of the groups involved; the machinery of enforcement of such political rights was as incomplete as that of the League of Nations.

Under such conditions the genocide policy begun by Germany on its own Jewish citizens in 1933 was considered as an internal problem which the German state, as a sovereign power, should handle without interference by other states.

Although the Hague regulations were concerned with the protection of civilians under control of military occupants, they did not foresee all the ingenious and scientific methods developed by Germany in this war.

Genocide is too disastrous a phenomenon to be left to fragmentary regulation. There must be an adequate mechanism for international cooperation in the punishment of the offenders. The

26

GENOCIDE IN ARMENIA

The Turkish plan was simple: extermination of the Armenians. And effective: by the time the mass killings of 1915 had concluded, a million and a half Armenians had died. This genocide did not end Armenian suffering....

Vigen Guroian, "Armenian Genocide and Christian Experience – Editors' note," **Cross Currents,** Fall 1991.

crime of genocide includes the following elements: The intent of the offenders is to destroy or degrade an entire national, religious, or racial group by attacking the individual members of that group. This attack is a serious threat either to life, liberty, health, economic existence, or to all of them. The offenders may be representatives of the state or of organized political or social groups.

Liability should be fixed upon individuals both as to those who give orders and to those who execute these orders. The offender should be precluded from invoking as his defense the plea that he had been acting under the law of his country, since acts of genocide should be declared contrary to international law and morality. Since the consequences of genocide are international in their implications the repression of genocide should be internationalized. The culprit should be liable not only in the country in which the crime was committed, but in the country where he might be apprehended. The country where he is found may itself try him or extradite him. Since a country which makes a policy of genocide cannot be trusted to try its own offenders, such offenders should be subject to trial by an international court. Eventually, there should be established a special chamber for international crimes within the framework of the existing International Tribunal of Justice.

The crime of genocide should be incorporated into the penal codes of all states by international treaty, giving them a legal basis upon which they could act.

Germany has reminded us that our science and our civilization have not expunged barbarism from the human animal. They have merely armed it with more efficient instruments. We must call upon the resources of all our social and legal institutions to protect our civilization against the onslaught of this wanton barbarism in generations to come.

READING

3

ORDINARY GERMANS, EXTRAORDINARY ANTISEMITISM

Daniel J. Goldhagen

Daniel Jonah Goldhagen is Assistant Professor of Government and Social Studies at Harvard University and an Associate of Harvard's Minda de Gunzburg Center for European Studies. His doctoral dissertation, which is the basis for his book, Hitler's Willing Executioners: Ordinary Germans and the Holocaust, *was awarded the American Political Science Association's 1994 Gabriel A. Almond Award for the best dissertation in the field of comparative politics.*

■ POINTS TO CONSIDER

1. According to Goldhagen, what is one of the primary weaknesses of Holocaust scholarship?

2. Who were the perpetrators of the Holocaust? Why is it important to study this?

3. Assess the author's contention that the Holocaust is the defining feature of German society during the Nazi period.

4. Describe Goldhagen's criticism of conventional explanations of the Holocaust.

5. Identify the central causal agent of the Holocaust, according to the author. Do you agree with this?

Not economic hardship, not the coercive means of a totalitarian state, not social psychological pressure... but ideas about Jews that were pervasive in Germany, and had been for decades, induced ordinary Germans to kill unarmed, defenseless Jewish men, women, and children by the thousands, systematically and without pity.

During the Holocaust, Germans extinguished the lives of six million Jews and, had Germany not been defeated, would have annihilated millions more....

Explaining the Holocaust is the central intellectual problem for understanding Germany during the Nazi period. All the other problems combined are comparatively simple. How the Nazis came to power, how they suppressed the left, how they revived the economy, how the state was structured and functioned, how they made and waged war are all more or less ordinary, "normal" events, easily enough understood. But the Holocaust and the change in sensibilities that it involved "defies" explanation....

EXECUTORS OF THE HOLOCAUST

Yet until now the perpetrators, the most important group of people responsible for the slaughter of European Jewry, excepting the Nazi leadership itself, have received little concerted attention in the literature that describes the events and purports to explain them. Surprisingly, the vast literature on the Holocaust contains little on the people who were its executors. Little is known of who the perpetrators were, the details of their actions, the circumstances of many of their deeds, let alone their motivations. A decent estimate of how many people contributed to the genocide, of how many perpetrators there were, has never been made. Certain institutions of killing and the people who manned them have hardly been treated or not at all. As a consequence of this general lack of knowledge, all kinds of misunderstandings and myths about the perpetrators abound....

These people were overwhelmingly and most importantly Germans. While members of other national groups aided the Germans in their slaughter of Jews, the commission of the Holocaust was primarily a German undertaking. Non-Germans were not essential to the perpetration of the genocide, and they did not supply the drive and initiative that pushed it forward. To

Illustration by Kitty Kennedy. Reprinted with permission.

be sure, had the Germans not found European (especially, Eastern European) helpers, then the Holocaust would have unfolded somewhat differently, and the Germans would likely not have succeeded in killing as many Jews. Still, this was above all a German enterprise; the decisions, plans, organizational resources, and the majority of its executors were German. Comprehension and explanation of the perpetration of the Holocaust therefore requires an explanation of the Germans' drive to kill Jews. Because what can be said about the Germans cannot be said about any other nationality or about all of the other nationalities combined — namely no Germans, no Holocaust — the focus here is appropriately on the German perpetrators....

DEFINING FEATURE OF GERMAN SOCIETY

The study of the perpetrators further demands a reconsideration, indeed a reconceiving, of the character of German society during its Nazi period and before. The Holocaust was the defining aspect of Nazism, but not only of Nazism. It was also the defining feature of German society during its Nazi period. No significant aspect of German society was untouched by anti-Jewish policy; from the economy to society, to politics, to culture, from cattle farmers to merchants, to the organization of small towns, to lawyers, doctors, physicists, and professors. No analysis of German society, no understanding or characterization of it, can be made without placing the persecution and extermination of the Jews at its center. The program's first parts, namely the systematic exclusion of Jews from German economic and social life, were carried out in the open, under approving eyes, and with the complicity of virtually all sectors of German society, from the legal, medical, and teaching professions, to the churches, both Catholic and Protestant, to the gamut of economic, social, and cultural groups and associations.[1] Hundreds of thousands of Germans contributed to the genocide and the still larger system of subjugation that was the vast concentration camp system. Despite the regime's half-hearted attempts to keep the genocide beyond the view of most Germans, millions knew of the mass slaughters.[2] Hitler announced many times, emphatically, that the war would end in the extermination of the Jews.[3] The killings met with general understanding, if not approval. No other policy (of similar or greater scope) was carried out with more persistence and zeal, and with fewer difficulties, than the genocide, except perhaps the War itself. The Holocaust defines not only the history of Jews during the middle of the twentieth century but also the history of Germans. While the Holocaust changed Jewry and Jews irrevocably, its commission was possible, I argue, because Germans had already been changed. The fate of the Jews may have been a direct, which does not, however, mean an inexorable, outgrowth of a worldview shared by the vast majority of the German people....

ANTISEMITISM CAUSED THE HOLOCAUST

This revision calls for us to acknowledge what has for so long been generally denied or obscured by academic and non-academic interpreters alike: Germans' antisemitic beliefs about Jews were the central causal agent of the Holocaust. They were the central causal agent not only of Hitler's decision to annihilate European Jewry (which is accepted by many) but also of the perpetrators' willingness to kill and to brutalize Jews. [A]ntisemitism moved many thousands of "ordinary" Germans — and would have moved millions more, had they been appropriately positioned — to slaughter Jews. Not economic hardship, not the coercive means of a totalitarian state, not social psychological pressure, not invariable psychological propensities, but ideas about Jews that were pervasive in Germany, and had been for decades, induced ordinary Germans to kill unarmed, defenseless Jewish men, women, and children by the thousands, systematically and without pity....

The conventional explanations *assume* a neutral or condemnatory attitude on the part of the perpetrators towards their

DEPORTATION TO TREBLINKA

In June 1942 placards bearing the following notice were posted on the walls of Warsaw: "Persons not employed in a German firm or the Jewish Community Administration are subject to immediate deportation from the ghetto; the able-bodied will be given employment." About the place of deportation, nothing was known except that it was in the East. Next to the new posters there immediately appeared "Help Wanted" advertisements of German firms. The factories, stores, and workshops owned by the Jews had been turned over to German administrators; thus a great number of new German firms had been created. People paid fantastic sums (from five to twenty thousand zlotys, $1,000 to $4,000, per person) to find employment in a German firm and thus escape deportation. Those who still had anything to sell converted it into cash. But those who had no funds were doomed.

Excerpted from an article by Samuel Rajzman submitted for the U.S. House Committee on Foreign Affairs, 22 March 1945.

actions....They *assume* and imply that inducing people to kill human beings is fundamentally no different from getting them to do any other unwanted or distasteful task. Also, none of the conventional explanations deems the *identity* of the victims to have mattered. The conventional explanations imply that the perpetrators would have treated any other group of intended victims in exactly the same way. That the victims were Jews — according to the logic of these explanations — is irrelevant....

CONCLUSION

My explanation — which is new to the scholarly literature on the perpetrators[4] — is that the perpetrators, "ordinary Germans," were animated by antisemitism, by a particular *type* of antisemitism that led them to conclude that the Jews *ought to die.*[5] The perpetrators' beliefs, their particular brand of antisemitism, though obviously not the sole source, was, I maintain, a most significant and indispensable source of the perpetrators' actions and must be at the center of any explanation of them. Simply put, the perpetrators, having consulted their own convictions and morality and having judged the mass annihilation of Jews to be right, did not *want* to say "no."...

NOTES FOR READING THREE

[1] This is discussed in Chapter 3, Daniel J. Goldhagen, *Hitler's Willing Executioners: Ordinary Germans and the Holocaust* (New York: Alfred A. Knopf, 1996).

[2] See Hans-Heinrich Wilhelm, "The Holocaust in National-Socialist Rhetoric and Writings: Some Evidence Against the Thesis that Before 1945 Nothing Was Known about the 'Final Solution,'" *YVS* 16 (1984): pp. 95-127; and Wolfgang Benz, "The Persecution and Extermination of the Jews in the German Consciousness," in John Milfull, ed., *Why Germany? National Socialist Anti-Semitism and the European Context* (Providence: Berg Publishers, 1993), pp. 91-104, esp. 97-98.

[3] See, for example, Max Domarus, *Hitler: Speeches and Proclamations, 1932-1945* (London: I.B. Tauris, 1990), vol. I, p. 41; and C.C. Aronsfeld, *The Text of the Holocaust: A Study of the Nazis' Extermination Propaganda, from 1919-1945* (Marblehead, Mass.: Micah Publications, 1985), pp. 34-36.

[4] A partial exception is the acknowledgment by Herbert Jäger, *Verbrechen unter totalitärer Herrschaft: Studien zur nationalsozialistischen Gewaltkriminalität* (Olton: Walter-Verlag, 1967), that some percentage of the perpetrators acted out of ideological conviction (pp. 62-64). Jäger, however, does not believe that it was ideological conviction that moved most of the perpetrators (see pp. 76-78). On the whole, as the book's title, *Crimes under Totalitarian Domination*, suggests, Jäger accepts the 1950s totalitarian model of Germany during the Nazi period (see pp. 186-208), employing concepts such as "totalitarian mentality" (totalitäre Geisteshaltung) (p. 186). This model — wrong in the most fundamental of ways and which continues to obscure for many the substantial freedom and pluralism that actually existed within German society — consistently misdirects Jäger's analysis, which in many ways is rich and insightful. For revisions and critiques of the totalitarian model's applicability to Germany during the Nazi period and of the general issues and debates in classifying Nazism, see Kershaw, *The Nazi Dictatorship*, pp. 17-39. Hans Safrian, in the introduction to his recent study of those who worked under Adolf Eichmann to deport European Jewry to their deaths, has also called into question the historical consensus that antisemitism did not motivate the perpetrators, though he fails to develop this notion much beyond asserting it. See *Die Eichmann-Männer* (Vienna: Europaverlag, 1993), pp. 17-22.

[5] Others have of course recognized and emphasized the importance of political ideology and antisemitism for the Nazi leadership's decision to undertake the total extermination of the Jews. For a wide-ranging discussion of this issue, see Eberhard Jäckel and Jürgen Rohwer, eds., *Der Mord an den Juden im Zweiten Weltkrieg: Entschlussbildung und Verwirklichung* (Stuttgart: Deutsche Verlags-Anstalt, 1985); Lucy Dawidowicz, *The War Against the Jews, 1933-1945* (New York: Bantam Books, 1975); Gerald Fleming, *Hitler and the Final Solution* (Berkeley: University of California Press, 1984), and Saul Friedländer's introduction to the book; and Klaus Hildebrand, *The Third Reich* (London: Allen & Unwin, 1984). Those who do take this position, however, either have not looked at the perpetrators or have denied that the perpetrators as a group were themselves moved by similar cognitions. Marrus, citing approvingly Hans Mommsen, speaks for the historical consensus in his historiographic *The Holocaust in History:* "Antisemitic indoctrination is plainly an insufficient answer, for we know [sic] that many of the officials involved in the administration of mass murder did not come to their tasks displaying intense antisemitism. In some cases, indeed, they appear to have had no history of anti-Jewish hatred and to have been coldly uninvolved with their victims" (p. 47). Erich Goldhagen is an exception to this general consensus, and although he has not published on the subject, he has emphasized in his course lectures and in our many conversations precisely the point being made here. Thus, while my claim might not sound so novel to some, it actually stands in contradiction to the existing literature.

33

READING

4

ORDINARY GERMANS, EXTRAORDINARY CONDITIONS

Victoria J. Barnett

Victoria J. Barnett works with the Churches' Center on Theology and Public Policy in Washington, D.C. Her most recent book is Bystanders: Conscience and Complicity during the Holocaust *(Greenwood Press, 1999). She is editor of the Washington, D.C.-based publication* The Shalom Papers: A Journal of Theology and Public Policy. *She is the translator of the forthcoming revised and unabridged version of Eberhard Bethge's noted biography of Dietrich Bonhoeffer.*

■ **POINTS TO CONSIDER**

1. Describe Barnett's opinion of Daniel Goldhagen's thesis.

2. According to the author, when do theories about nationalism and conformity fall short?

3. Examine Barnett's view about antisemitism and its role in the Holocaust. Contrast this to Goldhagen's view.

4. Evaluate the author's contention that it is "more comforting to believe Goldhagen's version" of the Holocaust explanation.

Excerpted from Victoria J. Barnett, "Why Did They Do It? Nazis and Ordinary Germans," **The Christian Century** 16 October 1996: 974-7. Copyright 1996 Christian Century Foundation. Reprinted by permission from the 16 OCTOBER 1996 issue of **The Christian Century.**

Even educated people, caught in the maelstrom of certain events, can lose or relinquish control of their laws, lives and institutions to the state. In the process, prejudices considered "harmless" assume new force.

Scholars who write about the Holocaust must straddle a line between the often conflicting demands of historical objectivity and moral passion. This is difficult not only because the Holocaust arouses such intense emotions but because what we can know about it is limited. We know a great deal about what happened, who was responsible, and who was victimized. But the hundreds of books on the topic have not diminished what Primo Levi called "the gray zone," that region of haunting questions about human behavior that cannot be answered with certainty. How could the highest achievements of human civilization — law, religion, diplomacy — so profoundly fail to stop this evil? How could ordinary human beings — people presumably raised to distinguish right from wrong, people with families of their own — participate in the vicious slaughter of powerless men, women and children?

BYSTANDERS, BUREAUCRATS, AND ENTHUSIASTIC PARTICIPANTS

Daniel Goldhagen answers this question by claiming that Germans—not as Nazis or as SS members, but as Germans — were driven by an "exterminationist antisemitism" that pervaded German culture long before the rise of Adolf Hitler. The result, writes Goldhagen, was that the murder of the European Jews was virtually preordained. It was "the defining feature of German society" under Nazism: "No analysis of German society, no understanding or characterization of it, can be made without placing the persecution and extermination of the Jews at its center." German antisemitism — not the chaos of the Weimar years, nationalism, public indifference, fear, subservience to authority, conformism or other factors often cited — was the "central causal agent of the Holocaust." The genocide of the Jews, Goldhagen concludes, was an endeavor in which most Germans enthusiastically participated....

It is easy to forget — particularly when we talk about "bystanders," or examine the Nazi bureaucrats who were far removed from the consequences of their activities — that there were thousands of individuals who personally tortured and murdered people with apparent conviction and enthusiasm. Goldhagen is right when he says that theories about nationalism or conformity fall short in explaining such behavior.

But by attributing this phenomenon solely to German cultural antisemitism, Goldhagen evades the deeper questions about the roots of such behavior, especially in extreme circumstances like wartime or under a dictatorship. He has decided to talk not about human behavior but about German behavior. One can't even study the Germans as one would study other people, he writes early in the book; the Germans are "unique" and must be approached as an anthropologist would approach a heretofore undiscovered tribe....

GERMAN ANTISEMITISM

The antisemitism in Christian, German and European culture was a very significant factor, although not the only factor, in what happened to the Jews under Nazism. Antisemitism and contempt for the Judaic tradition has certainly existed in the Christian church for centuries. It has often erupted into violent attacks upon Jews, instigated, in some cases, by church leaders. But it is hardly a core Christian teaching....

Most contemporary and historical accounts show a more ambivalent public reaction to the Nazi racial measures than Goldhagen portrays, on the part of both German Jews and non-Jews. Some historians contend that antisemitism was actually a negligible factor in popular support for the Nazi regime and, just like Goldhagen, they can cite evidence to support their case. For example, the U.S. consul in Leipzig reported a widespread lack of popular enthusiasm there for the April 1, 1933, boycott of Jewish businesses, and numerous reports about the reaction to the 1938 *Kristallnacht* (including the opposition Sopade reports, which Goldhagen uses elsewhere) suggested that the assault on Jewish establishments had "seriously damaged the prestige of the regime." Goldhagen's view that German society was permeated by "eliminationist" antisemitism even before 1933 is belied further by the fact that German Jews considered themselves assimilated....

Ironically, by focusing exclusively on "eliminationist antisemitism" as the German norm, Goldhagen ignores the insidious nature of the prejudice that did exist. The question we face in looking at the perpetrators of the final solution is the extent to which they were driven by antisemitism or by something else....Was it antisemitism alone that moved Germans from passive prejudice to active murder? If not, what other factors were involved? If we combat prejudice in individuals, will this affect their behavior as a group or in extreme situations? Or will all such attempts be futile, as Reinhold Niebuhr suggested in *Moral Man and Immoral Society* when he wrote about "the brutal nature of all human collectives"?

INTERNATIONAL INDIFFERENCE

The historical evidence suggests that a number of factors enabled the genocide of the European Jews to occur. Moreover, it is clear that a great many other people — the populations of the occupied countries and foreign officials, for example — behaved like "ordinary Germans." They either participated in killing Jews or they looked away. "The road to Auschwitz," as Ian Kershaw has written, "was built by hate, but paved with indifference."

Perhaps this "indifference" is different from that of a villager watching Jews led away or of a German soldier contemplating the bodies of his victims. But, given the widespread nature of this phenomenon during the Nazi reign of terror, it is difficult to attribute all of it to German antisemitism....

[F]aced with the increasing desperation of European Jews, the rest of the world shut its doors to emigrants. Confronted by the Nazi forces' open brutality toward Jews in occupied countries, very few non-Germans distinguished themselves by acts of resistance or rescue. Collaboration, complicity and "indifference" were the norm.

It should be possible to condemn German antisemitism and still acknowledge the broader complexity of what happened. Something did indeed go terribly wrong in German society between 1933 and 1945, and it is obvious that the foundation was laid beforehand. But if we truly want to understand what happened—or to draw any lessons from it for ourselves—we have to confront the issues that arise in the gray zone.

Oddly, it might be more comforting to believe Goldhagen's version than to look for more complex answers: perhaps this explains the resonance his book has found among some readers and reviewers. By arguing that the genocide of the Jews was intentional and planned, the logical outcome of German culture, Goldhagen resolves the most troubling aspect of the Holocaust: the problem of how well-fed, educated, civilized human beings can turn into monsters. Goldhagen has an explanation for everything, and it all fits together neatly in a terrible kind of logic.

MORAL REFLECTION

But if it were really that easy to explain, I don't think that the Holocaust would continue to trouble people the way it has. The notion of a German *Sonderweg* [unique historical trajectory] has been discredited not just by ongoing historical research, but by deeper moral reflection. It has become clear that it is possible for history to overrun people. Even educated people, caught in the maelstrom of certain events, can lose or relinquish control of their laws, lives and institutions to the state. In the process, prejudices considered "harmless" assume new force, and people conform to patterns of thought and behavior that they once would have considered unimaginable....

READING

5

HOLOCAUST DENIAL: RECOGNIZING THE UNIQUE FATE OF THE JEWS

Lucy S. Dawidowicz

The late Lucy Dawidowicz was an historian of the Holocaust and a regular contributor to Commentary *magazine. Some of Dawidowicz' most important works include* The War Against the Jews 1933-45 *and* The Holocaust and Historians.

■ **POINTS TO CONSIDER**

1. Describe how the Nazis asserted their rule over the civilians of occupied territories.

2. Summarize the Nazi racial hierarchy, according to Dawidowicz.

3. Compare and contrast the fate of the Jews and Gypsies under National Socialism.

4. Summarize the means the Germans used to annihilate the Jews.

5. Evaluate Dawidowicz' contention that the Holocaust is distinct, not universal.

Reprinted by permission of the publisher from *THE HOLOCAUST AND HISTORIANS* by Lucy S. Dawidowicz, Cambridge, Mass: Harvard University Press, Copyright © 1981 by the President and Fellows of Harvard College.

*To make Auschwitz serve as the paradigm for univer-
sal evil is in effect to deny the historical reality that
the German dictatorship had a specific intent in
murdering the Jews.*

It has been estimated that at least 35 million persons, perhaps
even as many as 50 million, were killed during the Second World
War in all theaters of operation in Europe, Africa, Asia, and the
South Pacific, on land, on sea, and in the air. They were combatants and civilians, men, women, and children, killed on the
battlefields and at home. Among some European peoples the
statistics of the killed were so immense as to depress the statistics
of those to be born in the next generation....

DEATH IN WAR

Poland ranks second [to the former Soviet Union] in the number
of war losses. The Bureau of War Indemnities of the Polish
People's Republic issued official figures of Poland's wartime losses, estimating a total of 6,028,000 deaths, about 22 percent of the
prewar population.[1] (If the Jewish losses are computed separately,
the number is about three million, or 12.5 percent of the Polish
population.)...

Even if these figures are high, as several Polish scholars
acknowledge privately, the Poles did suffer great losses, for the
German military and civilian occupation authorities dealt ruthless-
ly with the Polish population....

All over Europe, wherever the Germans had the power, they
enforced their total rule by arresting masses of the civilian population whom they regarded as politically dangerous, socially harm-
ful, or economically expendable. The categories were diverse:
Communists, socialists, and other political opponents; outspoken
members of the clergy and especially Jehovah's Witnesses, who
refused to recognize the secular sovereignty of National
Socialism; prostitutes, homosexuals, perverts, and professional
criminals. To make room for all these prisoners, the National
Socialist regime constructed a vast network of concentration
camps. In time, to exploit the available human resources under
their control, the Germans developed a system of forced labor in
the camps, and in the later years of the War, when German
manpower needs were desperate, the slave labor of these prisoners from all over Europe became a staple of the German war

"Gate of Auschwitz." Illustration by Kitty Kennedy. Reprinted with permission.

economy. It has been estimated that over the years about 1,650,000 persons were incarcerated in these camps. Over a million of them died or were killed. Some died of "natural" causes: hunger, exhaustion, disease. Those who lingered, the ailing, the sick, and the dying, no longer able to work and consequently, in the Nazi view, no longer worth keeping alive, were sent to the gas chambers that nearly every camp maintained to dispose of what Hitler called the "useless eaters."[2]...

RACIAL HIERARCHY

In the hierarchy of Nazi racism, the "Aryans" were the superior race, destined to rule the world after the destruction of their racial archfoe, the Jews. The lesser races over whom the Germans would rule included the Slavs — Poles, Russians, Ukrainians.

It has been said that the Germans also planned to exterminate the Poles and the Russians on racial grounds since, according to Hitler's racial doctrine, Slavs were believed to be subhumans *(Untermenschen).* But no evidence exists that a plan to murder the Slavs was ever contemplated or developed. The German racists assigned the Slavs to the lowest rank of human life, from which the Jews were altogether excluded. The Germans thus looked upon Slavs as people not fit to be educated, not able to govern themselves, worthy only as slaves whose existence would be justified because they served their German masters. Hitler's racial policy with regard to the Slavs, to the extent that it was formulated, was "depopulation." The Slavs were to be prevented from procreating, except to provide the necessary continuing supply of slave laborers. Whether the Russians — or the other "non-Aryan" peoples — lived or died was, as Himmler once put it to his top SS officers, "a matter of indifference." In contrast, he justified and even extolled the murder of the Jews as "an unwritten and never-to-be-written page of glory" in German history.[3]

EUROPEAN GYPSIES

The European Gypsies, too, suffered enormous losses at the hands of the Germans, yet the National Socialist state had no clear-cut racial policy with regard to them. Hitler appears to have overlooked them in his racial thinking. The Germans regarded the Gypsies primarily as an antisocial element, consisting of thieves and vagrants, rather than as an alien racial group. When the National Socialist regime began to incorporate its racial ideas in legislation, the Ministry of Interior ordered investigations to be made as to whether Gypsies were racially fit to be educated. (The answer was no.) But not until August 1941 did the German bureaucracy make any systematic attempt to classify the Gypsies racially. At that time Nazi officials established two basic categories, dividing the native Gypsy tribes from the foreign ones. The native tribes were defined as those who had settled in Germany since the fifteenth century, and hence were entitled to citizenship and the protection of German law. Distinctions also began to be made between "pure" Gypsies and "part" Gypsies (offspring of marriages between Gypsies and Germans), classifications that were patterned on the Nuremberg Laws promulgated in 1935 and frequently refined and implemented. When the Nazis began in 1941 to formulate a racial policy with regard to the Gypsies, no agreement on the matter had been reached by the top Nazi leaders....

During the War, tens of thousands of Gypsies living in Germany, Austria, and other German-occupied countries were deported to camps in Poland, including Auschwitz. The statistics of the murdered Gypsies are gross estimates: of about one million Gypsies in the countries that fell under German control, nearly a quarter of them were murdered — machine-gunned or gassed.

THE JEWS: A SPECIAL CASE

The fate of the Jews under National Socialism was unique. They obsessed Hitler all his life and their presence in Germany, their very existence, preoccupied the policymakers of the German dictatorship. The *Judenfrage* — the question of the Jews — riveted all Germany. The age-old heritage of antisemitism, compounded of Christian prejudices, economic rivalries, and social envy, was fanned by Nazi racism. Every German city, town, and village applied itself to the Jews and the Jewish question with rampant violence and meticulous legalism....

The German dictatorship devised two strategies to conduct its war of annihilation against the Jews: mass shooting and mass gassing. Special-duty troops of the SS Security Service and Security Police, called *Einsatzgruppen,* were assigned to each of the German armies invading the Soviet Union. Following hard upon the armed forces and dependent upon them for basic services, the Einsatzgruppen were given the task of rounding up the Jews and killing them....

To systematize the murder of the rest of the European Jews the National Socialist state built six installations with large-scale gassing facilities and with crematoria for the disposal of the bodies. There were all located on Polish territory: Oswięcim (better known by its German name, Auschwitz), Belzec, Chelmno, Majdanek, Sobibór, and Treblinka. The technology applied here — discharging poison gas through shower-head vents in sealed chambers — was barely more sophisticated than the brute violence of the *Einsatzgruppen*. The logistics, however, were impressive, and in the three years during which these killing installations operated, about 3.5 million Jews from every country of Europe were murdered there.* (Approximately 1.5 million non-Jews were gassed in these camps, most at Auschwitz.)

Of the nine million Jews who lived in the countries of Europe that fell under German rule during the War, about six million—that is, two-thirds of all European Jews—were murdered. Their numbers and concentration in Eastern Europe and their uninterrupted cultural traditions there for a thousand years had rendered them the most vital Jewish community, whose creativity sustained Jews throughout the world. Though the Soviet Union suffered greater losses than the Jews in absolute figures, no other people anywhere lost the main body of its population and the fountainhead of its cultural resources. No other people was chosen for total extinction.

ENDS IN THEMSELVES

The deaths of the six million European Jews were not a byproduct of the War. The Jews did not die as a consequence of the indiscriminate reach of bombs or gunfire or of the unselective fallout of deadly weapons. Nor were they the victims of the cruel and brutal expediency that actuated the Nazis to kill the Soviet prisoners of war and the Polish elite. Those murders were intended as means to practical ends: they were meant to protect and to consolidate the position of the Germans as undisputed masters over Europe. The murder of the Jews and the destruction of Jewish communal existence were, in contrast, ends in themselves, ultimate goals to which the National Socialist state had dedicated itself.

To refer to the murder of the six million Jews as distinctive, as unique, is not an attempt to magnify the catastrophe that befell them nor to beg tears and pity for them. It is not intended to minimize the deaths of the millions of non-Jews that the Germans brought about, or to underplay the immeasurable and unendurable suffering of Russians, Poles, Gypsies, and other victims of the German murder machine. To speak of the singularity of the murder of the six million European Jews is not to deny the incontestable fact that the gas chambers extinguished without discrimi-

*In computing the statistics of the six million murdered Jews, it is estimated that in addition to the two million killed by the *Einsatzgruppen* and the 3.5 million in the gas chambers, about 500,000 died in the ghettos of Eastern Europe of hunger, disease, and exhaustion, and as victims of random terror and reprisals.

nation all human life. The murder of the six million Jews stands apart from the deaths of the other millions, not because of any distinctive fate that the individual victims endured, but because of the differentiative intent of the murderers and the unique effect of the murderers....

UNIVERSALIZED HOLOCAUST

It was to be anticipated that Auschwitz would become a metaphor and a paradigm for evil. How could it be otherwise? But what was unexpected was the occasional attempt to turn Auschwitz into a metaphor for the "ecumenical nature" of the evil that was committed there or to render the murder of the Jews as mere atrocity, sheer blood lust. What was unexpected was the failure to understand — or to acknowledge — that the evil was not ecumenical, that the killing was not blood lust for its own sake, but that the evil and killing were specifically directed against particular victims. To make Auschwitz serve as the paradigm for universal evil is in effect to deny the historical reality that the German dictatorship had a specific intent in murdering the Jews....*

By subsuming the Jewish losses under a universal or ecumenical classification of human suffering, one can blur the distinctiveness of Jewish fate and consequently one can disclaim the presence of antisemitism, whether it smolders in the dark recesses of one's own mind or whether it operates in the pitiless light of history. Therefore, one can feel free to reject political or moral responsibility for the consequences of that antisemitism....

*I am not here referring to those who altogether deny that the European Jews were annihilated, like Arthur R. Butz, author of an overtly antisemitic work called *The Hoax of the Twentieth Century*. Those people are outright Nazis or Nazi apologists.

NOTES FOR READING FIVE

[1] Jan Szafranski, "Poland's Losses in World War II," *1939-1945: War Losses in Poland,* Studies and Monographs (Poznán: Zachodnia Agencja Prasowa, 1960), esp. pp. 44-49.

[2] Central Commission for the Investigation of German Crimes in Poland, *German Crimes in Poland,* I (Warsaw, 1946), esp. 45. 45. For the variety of reasons that brought people to Auschwitz see Bernd Naumann, *Auschwitz: A Report on the Proceedings Against Robert Karl Ludwig Mulka and Others Before the Court at Frankfurt* (London: Pall Mall, 1966). For an excellent critical analysis of available statistics on concentration camp population, turnover, and mortality see Joseph Billig, *Les Camps de Concentration dans L'Economie du Reich Hitlérien* (Paris: Presses Universitaires de France, 1973), pp. 68-99.

[3] Helmut Krausnick, "Denkschrift Himmlers über die Behandlung der Fremdvölkischen im Osten," *Vierteljahrshefte für Zeitgeschichte,* 5 (1957), 197. For Himmler's speech, October 4, 1943, see Lucy S. Dawidowicz, ed., *A Holocaust Reader* (New York: Behrman House, 1976), pp. 131-132.

[4] The most reliable source about the fate of the Gypsies under the Nazis is Donald Kenrick and Grattan Puxon, *The Destiny of Europe's Gypsies* (London: Chatto Heineman for Sussex University Press, 1972), esp. pp. 83-99, 144-149, and the statistics on pp. 183-184.

[5] For statistics on the European Jews killed see Dawidowicz, *The War Against the Jews,* pp. 402-403.

[6] See William Styron, "Auschwitz's Message," *New York Times,* June 25, 1974, and his essay "Hell Reconsidered," *New York Review of Books.* June 29, 1978, which appeared, in somewhat different form, as an introduction to the paperback edition of Richard L. Rubenstein, *The Cunning of History* (New York: Harper Torchbook, 1978). See also Kurt Vonnegut, Jr., *Slaughterhouse-Five* (New York: Dell, 1971), p. 96, where he provides an indiscriminate list of victims of the Nazi state: "Jews and Gypsies, and Fairies and Communists, and Other Enemies of the State."

READING

6

HOLOCAUST DENIAL: RECLAIMING THE INVISIBLE VICTIMS

Ward Churchill

Ward Churchill is an enrolled Keetoowah Cherokee and is Professor of American Indian Studies with the Department of Ethnic Studies at the University of Colorado, Boulder. He has been a member of the American Indian Movement (AIM) since 1972 and has led the Colorado Chapter for over 15 years. He is the author of several books and writes extensively on Native American issues.

■ **POINTS TO CONSIDER**

1. Compare and contrast the fate of Jews and Gypsies, according to Churchill.

2. Evaluate Churchill's view of genocide. Does the author embrace a minimalist or maximalist view of genocide? (See Reading One.)

3. Why does the author believe Slavic peoples were also victims of the Holocaust?

4. Assess Churchill's argument to restore "invisible victims" to the Holocaust.

5. Does the author believe the Holocaust is unique? Explain.

Excerpted from Ward Churchill, *A Little Matter of Genocide: Holocaust and Denial in the Americas, 1492 to the Present,* San Francisco: City Lights Books, 1997. Copyright © 1997 by Ward Churchill. Reprinted by permission of CITY LIGHTS BOOKS.

The true human costs of Nazi genocide came to 26 million or more, six million of whom were Jews, a million or more of whom were Gypsies, and the rest mostly Slavs.

The costs of systematic assaults on truth and memory have often been high for those whose suffering is correspondingly downgraded or shunted into historical oblivion. This concerns not only the victims of the many genocides occurring outside the framework of Nazism, but also the non-Jews targeted for elimination within the Holocaust itself. Consider, for example, the example of the Sinti and Roma peoples (Gypsies, also called "Romani")....

RECLAIMING INVISIBLE VICTIMS

In their zeal to prevent what they call a "dilution" or "de-Judaization" of the Holocaust, Jewish exclusivists have habitually employed every device known to deniers to depict the *Porrajmos* (as the Holocaust is known in the Romani language; the Hebrew equivalent is *Shoah*) as having been something "fundamentally different" from the Holocaust itself. The first technique has been to consistently minimize Gypsy fatalities. Lucy Dawidowicz, for instance, when she mentions them at all, is prone to repeating the standard mythology that, "of about one million Gypsies in the countries that fell under German control, nearly a quarter of them were murdered." The point being made is that, while Gypsy suffering was no doubt "unendurable," it was proportionately far less than that of the Jews.[1]

Actually, as more accurate — or honest — demographic studies reveal, the Gypsy population of German-occupied Europe likely came to somewhere around two million in 1939.[2] Of these, it was known at least thirty years ago that between 500,000 and 750,000 died in camps such as Buchenwald, Neuengamme, Bergen-Belsen, Belzec, Chelmno, Majdanek, Sobibór, and Auschwitz. More recent research shows that there were as many as a million more Gypsies exterminated when the tolls taken by the *Einsatzgruppen,* antipartisan operations in Eastern Europe, and actions by Nazi satellite forces are factored in. One reason for this ambiguity in terms of how many Gypsies died at the hands of the Nazis, leaving aside the gross undercounting of their initial population, is that their executioners not infrequently tallied their dead in with the numbers of Jews killed (thus somewhat inflating estimations of the Jewish count while diminishing that of the Sinti and Roma). In sum, it is plain that the proportional loss of the Gypsies during the Holocaust was at least as great as that of the Jews, and quite probably greater.[3]

Be that as it may, exclusivists still contend that the Gypsies stand apart from the Holocaust because, unlike the Jews, they were "not marked for complete annihilation."[4] According to Richard Breitman, "The Nazis are not known to have spoken of the Final Solution of the Polish problem or the Gypsy problem."[5]...

THE GYPSY QUESTION

As concerns the Gypsies, [these claims] amount to a bold-faced lie. This is readily evidenced by Himmler's "Decree for Basic Regulations to Resolve the Gypsy Question as Required by the Nature of Race" of December 8, 1938, which initiated preparations for the "*complete extermination* of the Sinti and Romani" (emphasis added).[6] Shortly after this, in February 1939, a brief was circulated by Johannes Behrendt of the Nazi Office of Racial Hygiene in which it was stated that "all Gypsies should be treated as hereditarily sick; the only solution is elimination. The aim should be the elimination without hesitation of this defective population." Hitler himself is reported to have verbally ordered "the liquidation of all Jews, Gypsies and Communist political functionaries in the entire Soviet Union" as early as June 1940.[7] A year later, Obergruppenfuhrer Reinhard Heydrich, head of the Reich Main Security Office, followed up by instructing his *Einsatzcommandos* to "kill all Jews, Gypsies and mental patients" in the conquered areas of the East.[8]...

"Adolf Eichmann made the recommendation that the 'Gypsy Question' be solved simultaneously with the 'Jewish Question'...Himmler signed the order dispatching Germany's Sinti and Roma to Auschwitz on 16th December 1942. The 'Final Solution' of the 'Gypsy Question' had begun" at virtually the same moment it can be said to have really gotten underway for the Jews.[9] Indeed, Gypsies were automatically subject to whatever policies applied to Jews during the entire period of the Final Solution, pursuant to a directive issued by Himmler on December 24, 1941 (i.e., four months prior to the Wannsee Conference which set the full-fledged extermination program in motion).[10] Hence, there is no defensible way the fate of the Gypsies can be distinguished from that of the Jews....

RECOVERING THE HOLOCAUST

There should be no need to go into such detail in rejoining exclusivist denials of the genocides perpetrated against Slavic peoples within the overall framework of the Holocaust. However, a tracing of the general contours seems appropriate, beginning with the familiar assertion that "they were treated differently from the Jews, and none were marked out for total annihilation."[11] As Lucy Dawidowicz puts it, "It has been said that the Germans...planned to exterminate the Poles and Russians on racial grounds since, according to Hitler's racial doctrine, Slavs were believed to be subhumans [Untermenschen]. But no evidence exists that a plan to murder the Slavs was ever contemplated or developed."[12]

There is both a grain of truth and a bucketful of falsity imbedded in these statements. In other words, it is true that Slavs were not named in the Endlösung [Final Solution] sketched out for Gypsies and Jews during the 1942 Wannsee Conference. This clearly suggests that the last two groups were given a certain priority in terms of the completion of their "special handling," but it is not at all to say that Slavs weren't "marked out" to suffer essentially the same fate in the end. Presumably, the final phases of the Nazis' anti-Slavic campaigns would have gotten underway once those directed against the much smaller Jewish and Gypsy populations had been wrapped up. In any event, the idea that "no plan [for Slavic extermination] was ever contemplated or developed" is quite simply false.

As is abundantly documented, the Hitlerian vision of Lebensraumpolitik — the conquest of vast expanses of Slavic territory in Eastern Europe for "resettlement" by a tremendously enlarged Germanic population—entailed a carefully calculated policy of eliminating resident Slavs.[13] In the U.S.S.R. alone, this planned "depopulation" was expressly designed to reduce those within the intended area of German colonization from about 75 million to no more than 30 million.[14] This sizable "residue" was to be maintained for an unspecified period to serve as an expendable slave labor pool to build the infrastructure required to support what the Nazis deemed "Aryan" living standards.[15]...

Unlike the Gypsies and Jews, the Slavs were mostly organized in a way lending itself to military resistance. Consequently, planning for their decimation necessarily factored in attrition through military confrontation.[16]...

And, if the standard practice of including the deaths of Jewish partisan fighters in the total of six million Jews claimed by the Holocaust were applied equally to Slavs, then plainly the body-count of partisans should be as well.[17]...

A gross estimate of the results of Nazi genocide against the Slavs thus comes to somewhere between 15.5 and 19.5 million in the U.S.S.R., between 19.7 and 23.9 million when the Poles, Slovenes, Serbs, and others are added in....The true human costs of Nazi genocide came to 26 million or more, six million of whom were Jews, a million or more of whom were Gypsies, and the rest mostly Slavs. Only with these facts clearly in mind can we say that we have apprehended the full scope of the Holocaust, and have thereby positioned ourselves to begin to appreciate its real implications.

UNCOVERING THE HIDDEN HOLOCAUSTS

University of Hawaii historian David Stannard has summed up the means by which exclusivists attempt to avert such understanding. "Uniqueness advocates begin by defining genocide (or the Holocaust or the *Shoah*) in terms of what they already believe to be experiences undergone only by Jews. After much laborious research it is then 'discovered' — *mirabile dictu* — that the Jewish experience was unique. If, however, critics point out after a time that those experiences are not in fact unique, other allegedly unique experiences are invented and proclaimed. If not *numbers* killed, how about *percentage* of population destroyed? If not *efficiency* or *method* of killing, how about perpetrator *intentionality* (emphasis in original)?"[18]...

In restoring the Gypsies and Slavic peoples to the Holocaust itself, where they've always belonged, we not only exhume them from the black hole into which they've been dumped in their millions by Jewish exclusivism and neonazism alike, we establish ourselves both methodologically and psychologically to remember other things as well. Not only was the Armenian Holocaust a "true" genocide, the marked lack of response to it by the Western democracies was used by Adolf Hitler to reassure his cabinet that there would be no undue consequences if Germany were to

> ## PORRAJMOS (ROMA HOLOCAUST)
>
> The Gypsy and Jewish approaches to memory seem to veer in opposite directions....Jews have invested in seeing their past — especially the Holocaust — presented on a grand scale before the general publics among whom they live. Gypsy memory, in contrast, like much else of their culture, remains within the confines of the community; for most Roma, monuments, museums, movies, and miniseries about their history have little relevance....
>
> Jeffrey Shandler, "The Other Other," **Tikkun,** Sept./Oct. 1996.

perpetrate its own genocide(s). Not only were Stalin's policies in the Ukraine a genuine holocaust, the methods by which they were carried out were surely incorporated into Germany's *Generalplan Ost* just a few years later.[19] Not only was the Spanish policy of conscripting entire native populations into forced labor throughout the Caribbean, as well as much of South and Central America holocaustal, it served as a prototype for Nazi policies in Eastern Europe.[20] Not only were U.S. "clearing" operations directed against the indigenous peoples of North America genocidal in every sense, they unquestionably served as a conceptual/practical mooring to which the whole Hitlerian rendering of *Lebensraumpolitik* was tied.

In every instance, the particularities of these prior genocides — each of them unique unto itself — serve to inform our understanding of the Holocaust. Reciprocally, the actualities of the Holocaust serve to illuminate the nature of these earlier holocausts. No less does the procedure apply to the manner in which we approach genocides occurring since 1945, those in Katanga, Biafra, Bangladesh, Indochina, Paraguay, Guatemala, Indonesia, Rwanda, Bosnia, and on and on. Our task is — *must* be — to fit *all* the various pieces together in such a way as to obtain at last a comprehension of the whole....

NOTES FOR READING SIX

[1] Lucy S. Dawidowicz, *The Holocaust and the Historians* (Cambridge: Harvard University Press, 1981) pp. 13-4.

[2] Ian Hancock, "'Uniqueness' of the Victims: Gypsies, Jews, and the Holocaust," *Without Prejudice,* Vol. 1, No. 2, 1988.

[3] Overall attrition of 65 percent — rather than the 25 percent allowed by Dawidowicz, Gilbert, and their cohorts — is a very conservative estimate; Ian Hancock, "Uniqueness, Gypsies, and Jews," in Bauer, et al., *Remembering for the Future, Vol. 2, Working Papers and Addenda* (Oxford: Pergamon Press, 1989) pp. 2017-25. Also see Sybil Milton, "The Context of the Holocaust," *German Studies Review,* Vol. 13, No. 2, 1990.

[4] Michael Berenbaum, *The World Must Know: The History of the Holocaust as Told in the United States Holocaust Memorial Museum* (Boston: Little, Brown, 1993) p. 2.

[5] Richard Breitman, *Architect of Genocide: Himmler and the Final Solution* (Hanover, NH: University Press of New England, 1991) p. 20.

[6] *Memorial Book,* op. cit. p. xiv.

[7] Breitman, *Architect of Genocide,* op. cit., p. 164.

[8] Benno Muller-Hill, *Murderous Science: Elimination by Scientific Selection of Jews, Gypsies and Others,* 1933-1945 (Oxford University Press, 1988) p. 59.

[9] Burleigh and Wipperman, *The Racial State: Germany 1933-1945* (Cambridge: Cambridge University Press, 1991) p. 125.

[10] Ian Hancock, "Responses to the Porrajmos," in Alan S. Rosenbaum, ed., *Is the Holocaust Unique? Perspectives on Comparative Genocide* (Boulder, CO: Westview Press, 1996) p. 51.

[11] Katz, *The Holocaust in Historical Context, Vol. 1: The Holocaust and Mass Death Before the Modern Age* (New York: Oxford University Press, 1992) p. 25.

[12] Dawidowicz, *The Holocaust and the Historians,* op. cit., p. 10.

[13] This includes the famous memorandum prepared by Hitler's adjutant, Col. Friedrich Hössbach, summarizing a high-level conference conducted on November 5, 1937, during which the Führer outlined his plans in great detail; *Trial of the Major War Criminals before the International Military Tribunal,* Vol. 25 (Nuremberg: International Military Tribunal, 1947-1949) pp. 402-13. Overall, see Robert Koehl, RKFDV: *German Resettlement and Population Policy, 1939-1945* (Cambridge: Harvard University Press, 1957); Ihor Kamensky, *Secret Nazi Plans for Eastern Europe: A Study of Lebensraum Policies* (New York: Bookman Associates, 1961); Norman Rich, *Hitler's War Aims: Ideology, the Nazi State, and the Course of Expansion* (New York: W.W. Norton, 1973).

[14] Systematic "depopulation" of a targeted group is, by definition, genocide; see Lemkin's *Axis Rule in Occupied Europe* (Washington, D.C.: Carnegie Endowment for International Peace, 1944). On Nazi depopulation plan objectives, see, e.g., Alexander Dallin, *German Rule in Occupied Russia, 1941-1945: A Study in Occupation Policies* (New York: Macmillan, 1957) esp. p. 278.

[15] The overall scheme was committed to writing under the title "Generalplan Ost" (General Plan East) in early 1942; "Der Generalplan Ost," *Viertjahrshefte fuer Zeitgeschichte,* No. 6 (1958), No. 1 (1960).

[16] These come within the scope of "Fall Barbarossa," the plan for the invasion of the Soviet Union. See, e.g., the so-called "Oldenburg Protocol" of March 29, 1941; Fieldmarshall Wilhelm Keitel's May 13, 1941, memorandum entitled "On the Military Jurisdiction in the Region of 'Barbarossa' and on Special Military Powers"; and the directive "Twelve Commandments for German Behavior in the East and for Treatment of Russians" of June 1, 1941; all in *Nazi Conspiracy and Aggression,* Vol. 6 (Washington, D.C.: U.S. Government Printing Office, 1946).

[17] Reubin Ainsztein, *Jewish Resistance in Nazi-Occupied Eastern Europe* (New York: Barnes & Noble, 1974); Lucien Steinberg, *The Jews Against Hitler (Not Like a Lamb)* (London: Gordon & Cremonesi, 1978); Isaiah Trunk, *Jewish Responses to Nazi Persecution* (New York: Scarborough Books, 1982).

[18] David E. Stannard, "The Politics of Holocaust Scholarship: Uniqueness as Denial," in Alan S. Rosenbaum, ed., *Is the Holocaust Unique?* (op. cit.).

[19] Robert Conquest, *The Harvest of Sorrow* (New York: Oxford University Press, 1986). Commission on the Ukrainian Famine, Investigation of the Ukrainian Famine, 1932-1933: Report to Congress (Washington, D.C.: U.S. Government Printing Office, 1988).

[20] See, e.g., Juan A. Villamarin and Judith E. Villamarin, *Indian Labor in Colonial Spanish America* (Newark: University of Delaware Press, 1975); William L. Sherman, *Native Forced Labor in Sixteenth Century Central America* (Lincoln: University of Nebraska Press, 1979).

THE CONVENTION ON THE PREVENTION AND PUNISHMENT OF THE CRIME OF GENOCIDE

After its founding in 1945, one of the first issues addressed by the new international body, the United Nations (UN) was a binding international instrument to recognize the crime of genocide. Unsuccessful in persuading the inclusion of a genocide convention in the post-World War II Paris Peace Conference in 1945, Raphael Lemkin turned to the UN. Lemkin, the originator of the term genocide *(see Reading Two) convinced Cuba, Panama and India to propose a resolution making genocide a crime under international law. The resolution passed unanimously in 1946. The Convention on the Prevention and Punishment of the Crime of Genocide was adopted by the UN General Assembly 9 December 1948, and entered into effect 12 January 1951.*

■ **POINTS TO CONSIDER**

1. According to the Convention, what acts constitute genocide?

2. Describe the means of enforcement of the Convention.

3. Compare and contrast this definition of genocide with that of Raphael Lemkin (see Reading Two).

Articles of the Convention on the Prevention and Punishment of the Crime of Genocide, 1951, submitted for the Commission on Security and Cooperation in Europe (Hearing: Genocide in Bosnia - Herzegonvina 4) April 1995.

THE CONTRACTING PARTIES

Having considered the declaration made by the General Assembly of the United Nations in its resolution 96 (I) dated 11 December 1946 that genocide is a crime under international law, contrary to the spirit and aims of the United Nations and condemned by the civilized world.

Recognizing that at all periods of history genocide has inflicted great losses on humanity, and

Being convinced that, in order to liberate mankind from such an odious scourge, international co-operation is required.

Hereby agree as hereinafter provided:

ARTICLE I

The Contracting Parties confirm that genocide, whether committed in time of peace or in time of war, is a crime under international law which they undertake to prevent and to punish.

ARTICLE II

In the present Convention, genocide means any of the following acts committed with intent to destroy, in whole or in part, a national, ethnical, racial or religious group, as such:

(a) Killing members of the group;

(b) Causing serious bodily or mental harm to members of the group;

(c) Deliberately inflicting on the group conditions of life calculated to bring about its physical destruction in whole or in part;

(d) Imposing measures intended to prevent births within the group;

(e) Forcibly transferring children of the group to another group.

ARTICLE III

The following acts shall be punishable:

(a) Genocide;

(b) Conspiracy to commit genocide;

(c) Direct and public incitement to commit genocide;

(d) Attempt to commit genocide;

(e) Complicity in genocide.

ARTICLE IV

Persons committing genocide or any of the other acts enumerated in Article III shall be punished, whether they are constitutionally responsible rulers, public officials or private individuals.

ARTICLE V

The Contracting Parties undertake to enact, in accordance with their respective Constitutions, the necessary legislation to give effect to the provisions of the present Convention, and, in particular, to provide effective penalties for persons guilty of genocide or any of the other acts enumerated in Article III.

ARTICLE VI

Persons charged with genocide or any of the other acts enumerated in Article III shall be tried by a competent tribunal of the State in the territory of which the act was committed, or by such international penal tribunal as may have jurisdiction with respect to those Contracting Parties which shall have accepted its jurisdiction.

ARTICLE VII

Genocide and the other acts enumerated in Article III shall not be considered as political crimes for the purpose of extradition.

The Contracting Parties pledge themselves in such cases to grant extradition in accordance with their laws and treaties in force.

ARTICLE VIII

Any Contracting Party may call upon the competent organs of the United Nations to take such action under the Charter of the United Nations as they consider appropriate for the prevention and suppression of acts of genocide or any of the other acts enumerated in Article III.

ARTICLE IX

Disputes between the Contracting Parties relating to the interpretation, application or fulfillment of the present Convention, including those relating to the responsibility of a State for genocide or for any of the other acts enumerated in Article III, shall be submitted to the International Court of Justice at the request of any of the parties to the dispute.

ARTICLE X

The present Convention, of which the Chinese, English, French, Russian and Spanish texts are equally authentic, shall bear the date of 9 December 1948.

ARTICLE XI

The present Convention shall be open until 31 December 1949 for signature on behalf of any member of the United Nations and of any non-member State to which an invitation to sign has been addressed by the General Assembly.

The present Convention shall be ratified, and the instruments of ratification shall be deposited with the Secretary-General of the United Nations.

After 1 January 1950, the present Convention may be acceded to on behalf of any Member of the United Nations and of any non-member State which has received an invitation as aforesaid.

Instruments of accession shall be deposited with the Secretary-General of the United Nations.

ARTICLE XII

Any Contracting Party may at any time, by notification addressed to the Secretary-General of the United Nations, extend the application of the present Convention to all or any of the territories for the conduct of whose foreign relations that Contracting Party is responsible.

ARTICLE XIII

On the day when the first twenty instruments of ratification or accession have been deposited, the Secretary-General shall draw up a *proces-verbal* and transmit a copy thereof to each Member of the United Nations and to each of the non-member States contemplated in Article XI.

The present Convention shall come into force on the ninetieth day following the date of deposit of the twentieth instrument of ratification or accession.

Any ratification or accession effected, subsequent to the latter date shall become effective on the ninetieth day following the deposit of the instrument of ratification or accession.

ARTICLE XIV

The present Convention shall remain in effect for a period of ten years as from the date of its coming into force.

It shall thereafter remain in force for successive periods of five years for such Contracting Parties as have not denounced it at least six months before the expiration of the current period.

Denunciation shall be effected by a written notification addressed to the Secretary-General of the United Nations.

ARTICLE XV

If, as a result of denunciations, the number of Parties to the present Convention should become less than sixteen, the Convention shall cease to be in force as from the date on which the last of these denunciations shall become effective.

ARTICLE XVI

A request for the revision of the present Convention may be made at any time by any Contracting Party by means of a notification in writing addressed to the Secretary-General.

The General Assembly shall decide upon the steps, if any, to be taken in respect of such request.

ARTICLE XVII

The Secretary-General of the United Nations shall notify all Members of the United Nations and the non-member States contemplated in Article XI of the following:

(a) Signatures, ratifications and accessories received in accordance with Article XI;

(b) Notifications received in accordance with Article XII;

(c) The date upon which the present Convention comes into force in accordance with Article XIII;

(d) Denunciations received in accordance with Article XIV;

(e) The abrogation of the Convention in accordance with Article XV;

(f) Notifications received in accordance with Article XVI.

ARTICLE XVIII

The original of the present Convention shall be deposited in the archives of the United Nations.

A certified copy of the Convention shall be transmitted to each Member of the United Nations and to each of the non-member States contemplated in Article XI.

ARTICLE XIX

The present Convention shall be registered by the Secretary-General of the United Nations on the date of its coming into force.

A QUESTION OF GENOCIDE

This activity may be used as an individualized study guide for students in libraries and resource centers or as a discussion catalyst in small group and classroom discussions.

Much bloodshed and inhumanity accompanied the disintegration of the former Yugoslavia. In the Fall of 1998, after the bloody civil war in Bosnia, increased media attention surrounded the situation in Kosovo. The province, situated in southern Yugoslavia (Serbia proper), is the cradle, according to many Serbian people, of Serbian culture and contains many important Orthodox religious and cultural sites. However, the population of the province is overwhelmingly ethnically Albanian. In 1989, Yugoslav leader Slobodan Milosovic rescinded the semi-autonomous status of the province, increasing tension between ethnic Albanians and Serbs.

Frequent reports of atrocities committed against ethnic Albanians by Yugoslav authorities prompted the international community to push for a peace agreement. Under threat of NATO bombings, Milosovic refused to sign off on the conditions of the agreement with the Kosovo Liberation Army (KLA) at Ramboullet, France. NATO bombing of Kosovo and Serbia began in March 1999, promptly followed by the forced expulsion of hundreds of thousands of ethnic Albanians by Yugoslav authorities. NATO bombing ended in June, 1999.

Cries of genocide and Holocaust comparisons prompted popular support for bombing. But, did the actions in Kosovo taken by Yugoslav authorities constitute genocide? Author and Holocaust survivor Elie Weisel says, "Massive violations of human rights and the murder of political opponents, as horrible as they may be, are elements of genocide-in-the-making, but they do not constitute genocide" (*Newsweek* 12 April 1999).

Guidelines

1. Do brief research on the 1999 situation in Kosovo. Use sources in print journalism, as well as the worldwide web.

2. Write an essay explaining why or why not Kosovo is a genocide. Refer to the Genocide Convention (previous reading).

3. Explain your opinion of the NATO response to Kosovo.

CHAPTER 2

EUROPEAN COLONIALISM, INDIGENOUS AMERICANS AND GENOCIDE

READING

8

THE MOST HORRENDOUS HOLOCAUST IN HISTORY: THE POINT

Winona LaDuke

Winona LaDuke resides on the White Earth Reservation in northern Minnesota with her two children. A prominent Native American environmental activist, LaDuke's work began at an early age. She spoke before the United Nations at eighteen. Through her studies at Harvard, she researched the health impact of mining on the Navajo Reservation. Returning to the reservation after her studies, LaDuke took the job as school principal and became involved in a lawsuit to recover land taken by the U.S. government. After losing the lawsuit, she founded the White Earth Land Recovery Project. She also founded the Indigenous Women's Network. In 1996, she ran on the Green Party ticket with Ralph Nader for Vice President of the U.S.

■ POINTS TO CONSIDER

1. Why does LaDuke believe Columbus set genocide in motion?

2. Who is Bartolemé de las Casas?

3. Evaluate the legacy of Columbus.

4. Discuss the impact of industry and commerce on native peoples. How can this be genocidal? Use the Genocide Convention to support your view.

Excerpted from Winona LaDuke, "We Are Still Here," **Sojourners.** October 1991: 12-6. Reprinted with permission from **Sojourners,** 2401 15th Street NW, Washington, DC 20009; (202) 328-8842 / (800) 714-7474.

Columbus was a perpetrator of genocide, responsible for setting in motion the most horrendous holocaust to have occurred in the history of the world.

To "discover" implies that something is lost. Something was lost, and it was Columbus. Unfortunately, he did not discover himself in the process of his lostness. He went on to destroy peoples, land, and ecosystems in his search for material wealth and riches.

COLUMBUS, THE INDIGENOUS AND GENOCIDE

Columbus was a perpetrator of genocide, responsible for setting in motion the most horrendous holocaust to have occurred in the history of the world. Columbus was a slave trader, a thief, a pirate, and most certainly not a hero. To celebrate Columbus is to congratulate the process and history of the invasion.

The Taino, Arawak, and other indigenous peoples of the Caribbean, the first "hosts of Columbus," were systematically destroyed. Thirteen at a time they were hanged, in honor of the 12 Apostles and the Redeemer. Every man over 14 years of age was obliged to bring a quota of gold to the *conquistadors* every three months. Those who could not pay the tribute had their hands cut off "as a lesson." Most bled to death. The Taino leaders argued with the *conquistadors.* They pleaded that "with their thousands of people grow[ing] enough corn to feed many of the people of Europe — was that not enough of a tribute, of a payment?"

The *conquistadors* would not accept their tribute from the land. So the "idle" ships of the second voyage of Columbus were used to transport back 500 Indians to be slaves to the markets of Seville. The repression was so brutal that many of the Taino, Caribs, and Arawaks, faced with brutality and slavery at the hands of *conquistadors,* chose instead to commit mass suicide.

50 MILLION PERISH

Sixty years later, in 1552, the Catholic priest Bartolemé de las Casas declared that within the entire Western Hemisphere, a total of 50 million Indians had already perished in just over a half-century of Spanish invasion. Las Casas had been an eyewitness to some of the slaughter and depopulation caused by diseases accidentally introduced by the Spanish. In his protest of his own people's "abominable cruelties and detestable tyrannies," Las

Cartoon by John Jonik. Reprinted with permission.

Casas cried out that five million had died on the Caribbean islands and that 45 million had died on the mainland. (In 1492, in the Western Hemisphere there were 112,554,000 American Indians. By 1980, there were 28,264,000 American Indians.)

Although Columbus himself later returned to Europe in disgrace, his methods were subsequently used in Mexico, Peru, the Black Hills and Wounded Knee in South Dakota, and Sand Creek in Colorado. They are still being used in Guatemala and El Salvador, and in Indian territory from Amazonia to Pine Ridge in South Dakota. The invasion set into motion a process, thus far unabated. This has been a struggle over values, religions, resources, and, most important, land.

COLONIAL VALUES

The "Age of Discovery" marked the age of colonialism, a time when our land suddenly came to be viewed as "your land." While military repression is not in North American vogue (at least with the exception of the Oka-Mohawk uprising of the summer of 1990), today legal doctrines uphold that our land is your land, based ostensibly on the so-called "doctrine of discovery." This justifies in the white legal system the same dispossession of people from their land that is caused by outright military conquest. But in a "kinder, gentler world," it all appears more legal.

The reality is that the battering has been relentless. With each generation more land has been taken from indigenous peoples — either by force or by paper, but in no case with our consent. Today, Indian people in North America retain about four percent of their original land base — land called reservations in the United States or reserves in Canada.

And those remaining lands are facing a new assault. Underlying Indian reservations are approximately two-thirds of the uranium resources within the continental United States and one-third of all Western low-sulphur coal. Other lands include vast oil tracts (including that in the so-called Arctic National Wildlife Refuge — the last unexploited portion of the north shore of Alaska) and final stands of pristine water and unexploited old-growth timber. The statistics for Canada are much the same.

ECO-GENOCIDE

What we have is still what they want, whether it is EXXON, ARCO, Rio Tinto Zinc (the British mining giant), COGEMA (the French uranium company that is active in Dene and Cree lands in northern Saskatchewan), or lumber companies from Japan or North America. The North American onslaught is matched only by that in South and Central America, where remaining rain forests and resource-rich lands are greedily consumed by foreign multinationals and governments.

The rate of exploitation is astounding. In 1975, 100 percent of all federally produced uranium in the United States came from

Indian reservations, so that Indians were the fifth largest producers of uranium in the world. That same year, four of the ten largest coal strip mines in the United States were on Indian reservations. By 1985, Dene and Cree lands in Saskatchewan were producing more than one billion dollars (U.S.) worth of uranium annually for foreign multinationals.

An area the size of France in northern Quebec has been devastated by hydroelectric development in a huge James Bay project, which is the largest manipulation of a sub-arctic ecosystem in history. The lands flooded are those of the Cree and Inuit — two peoples who have lived there for 10,000 years or more in a carefully balanced way of life. Today, thousands more face relocation as new dams are proposed for European aluminum interests (who will locate in Quebec to secure cheap electricity) and American consumers. The devastation of the ecosystems and the people is relentless. In short, the problem or challenge posed is the invasion, and the reality is that it continues.

We understand that "to get to the rain forest, you must first kill the people," and that is why since 1900 one-third of all indigenous nations in the Amazon have been decimated, while during the same time one-quarter of the forest has disappeared. There is a direct relationship between how industrial society consumes land and resources and how it consumes peoples.

500 YEAR STRUGGLE

In the past 150 years, we have seen the extinction of more species than since the Ice Age. And since 1492, we have witnessed the extinction of more than 2,000 indigenous peoples from the Western Hemisphere. Where are the Wappo, the Takelma, the Natchez, and the Massachuset?...

Through it all, indigenous people will continue to struggle. It is this legacy of resistance that...is like a constant rumble of distant thunder, and it says through the wind, "We are alive. We are still here."

INDIANS LOST THE WAR: THE COUNTERPOINT

Jeffrey Hart

Jeffrey Hart is distinguished Professor of English at Dartmouth College. He writes a twice-weekly syndicated column and is a Senior Editor at The National Review. *In 1968, Hart took a leave from teaching to work with Ronald Reagan as a writer and consultant. He has been a speech writer for two presidents. Born in 1930 in New York City, Hart received his bachelor's and doctoral degrees from Columbia.*

■ POINTS TO CONSIDER

1. In your estimation, how would Hart respond to LaDuke's charge that Columbus perpetrated genocide? (See Reading Eight.)

2. Evaluate the author's various characterizations of Native Americans. Do you believe they are "harmless"?

3. Examine Hart's opinion about the term "Native American" itself.

4. Describe what led to the demise of Native Americans, according to Hart. What would have "prevented" their decline?

Excerpted from Jeffrey Hart, "Revisionists Can't Help Indians Win the War," **Conservative Chronicle,** 25 December 1996: 25. Reprinted with permission, King Feature Syndicate.

The Indians lost the long war because their overall culture and Stone Age tribal organization were inferior and could not prevail.

The schmaltzy idealization of the American Indian has become an industry. The actual American Indian of history has been lost in an orgy of civilization-bashing.

We have "Native American Studies" courses in the universities, commercial movies such as *Pocahontas* and notably now Ken Burns' nine-part PBS series, *The West.*

ANTI-EUROPEAN, ANTI-HISTORICAL

American culture has long idealized the Indian in harmless ways. In the Boy Scouts, I entered as a "Tenderfoot" and thought about Indians moving silently over dried leaves and paddling birch-bark canoes. I tried to make a fire with flint and twigs. The Indian has adorned our currency and given his name to cities and athletic teams.

But what we are now seeing is different. Those "Native American Studies" courses are almost always anti-European and also anti-historical.

Often, as in the Ken Burns documentary, the wish is explicit that the Indians had not been defeated and that America would revert to pre-Colonial times.

It amounts to a bogus wish that modern civilization did not exist. Of course that cannot be brought about. Pol Pot tried, and look at what happened.

For centuries before the Indians ever saw a white man, they slaughtered one another in bloody tribal warfare. When the Europeans arrived, there commenced a long war of about 150 years. The Indians lost decisively.

The Indians were by no means "native" to America. At the end of the Ice Age, they crossed from Siberia on a land bridge that existed between the continents. The Indians are Asians.

Then they worked their way down from what would become Alaska and encountered a resident people now known as "Mound Builders" because of the large earth structures they left. The nomadic warriors from Siberia extinguished the Mound Builders, and then fought each other for centuries.

The reasons why the Indians lost the long war against the European settlers were not mainly technological. Soon the Indians had muskets and horses, and later on rifles. They were excellent riders and fighters.

They could have formed a united army of some sort to do battle, but that was far beyond them. They were a Stone Age tribal people, the tribes hating one another as much or more than they hated the whites. (Look at Africa today.) In fact, the most warlike tribes, such as the Sioux, the Comanches and the Apaches, were so savage that other tribes often joined the whites against them.

WARLIKE TRIBES

Among the young braves of the warlike tribes, fighting was the most honored activity, and the only route to honor, booty and captured women. Any Indian chief with an impulse toward peace would have been regarded as an old woman and replaced. Similarly any chief who tried to form a coalition with other tribes.

The whites did not win because of rifles and horses, but through better organization and steadiness of purpose. The frontier advanced steadily against the nomads, farms were established and forts built to protect the settlers.

The Indians lost the long war because their overall culture and Stone Age tribal organization were inferior and could not prevail....

ASSIMILATION

[T]he Indians had another position besides fighting. They could have rejected tribalism and its ethos and assimilated to the 19th century Western civilization. Indeed many of them did, and their descendants today live among the rest of the Americans.

[Walter A.] McDougal has come up with a remarkable quotation I had not seen before. Writing to the Cheyenne Chief Lean Bear, Abraham Lincoln put the matter with his characteristic grace and realism:

"I really am not capable of advising you whether, in the providence of the Great Spirit, who is the Father of us all, it is for you to maintain the habits and customs of your race, or adopt a new model of life. I only say that I can see no way in which your race is to become as numerous and prosperous as the white race except by living as they do, by the cultivation of the earth."

So, the Indians lost the war. The Scottish Highlanders were destroyed after the Battle of Culloden in 1745 for the same reasons.

It is utterly frivolous to wish that the Indians had won.

One may blanche at the barbarities committed by both sides in what was usually guerrilla warfare, but that is the nature of guerrilla warfare.

History is not a videotape. There is no "reverse" button. Rome was overrun. The Aztecs lost. The Highlanders lost. The Indians lost. The Confederacy lost.

I doubt that Ken Burns would go to a witch doctor instead of a modern physician. The Indians had no written language and had not invented the wheel.

There comes a time when historical realism has to break in and when the kidding has to stop.

READING

10

GUATEMALAN GENOCIDE: THE POINT

Commission on Historical Clarification

The UN-sponsored Commission for Historical Clarification (CEH) was established through the Accord of Oslo 23 June 1994 to identify acts of violence connected with armed confrontation in Guatemala's civil war. On 29 December 1996, Peace Accords between the UNRG Revolutionary Movement and the Guatemalan Government were signed. The 3,500-page report documenting the human rights violations during Guatemala's 36-year war was released March 1999 by CEH.

■ POINTS TO CONSIDER

1. What does the CEH identify as the roots of armed confrontation?

2. Describe the effect of Cold War policies on Guatemala.

3. Explain the position of Mayan peoples in Guatemala during the war. How did the government view Mayans?

4. Evaluate the Commission's claim that acts of genocide were committed against the Mayan people.

Excerpted from the UN Commission on Historical Clarifications report "Guatemala: Memory of Silence," 1999, available at American Association for the Advancement of Science, hrdata.aaas.org/.

The State of Guatemala committed acts of genocide against Mayan people.

Guatemala is a country of contrasts and contradictions. Situated in the middle of the American continent, bathed by the waters of the Caribbean and the Pacific, its inhabitants live in a multiethnic, pluricultural and multilingual nation, in a State which emerged from the triumph of liberal forces in Central America. Guatemala has seen periods marked by beauty and dignity from the beginning of the ancient Mayan culture to the present day; its name has been glorified through its works of science, art, and culture; by men and women of honor and peace, both great and humble; by its Nobel Laureates for Literature and Peace. However, in Guatemala, pages have also been written of shame and infamy, disgrace and terror, pain and grief, all as a product of the armed confrontation among brothers and sisters. For more than 34 years, Guatemalans lived under the shadow of fear, death and disappearance as daily threats in the lives of ordinary citizens....

THE TRAGEDY OF THE ARMED CONFRONTATION

With the outbreak of the internal armed confrontation in 1962, Guatemala entered a tragic and devastating stage of its history, with enormous human, material and moral cost. In the documentation of human rights violations and acts of violence connected with the armed confrontation, the Commission for Historical Clarification (CEH) registered a total of 42,275 victims, including men, women and children. Of these, 23,671 were victims of arbitrary execution and 6,159 were victims of forced disappearance. Eighty-three percent of fully identified victims were Mayan and seventeen percent were Ladino.

Combining this data with the results of other studies of political violence in Guatemala, the CEH estimates that the number of persons killed or disappeared as a result of the fratricidal confrontation reached a total of over 200,000.

The Commission for Historical Clarification concludes that the structure and nature of economic, cultural and social relations in Guatemala are marked by profound exclusion, antagonism and conflict — a reflection of its colonial history. The proclamation of independence in 1821, an event prompted by the country's elite, saw the creation of an authoritarian State which excluded the majority of the population, was racist in its precepts and practices,

74

and served to protect the economic interests of the privileged minority. The evidence for this, throughout Guatemala's history, but particularly so during the armed confrontation, lies in the fact that the violence was fundamentally directed by the State against the excluded, the poor and above all, the Mayan people, as well as against those who fought for justice and greater social equality....

NATIONAL SECURITY DOCTRINE AND THE U. S.

The CEH recognizes that the movement of Guatemala towards polarization, militarization and civil war was not just the result of national history. The Cold War also played an important role. While anti-communism, promoted by the United States within the framework of its foreign policy, received firm support from right-wing political parties and from various other powerful actors in Guatemala, the United States demonstrated that it was willing to provide support for strong military regimes in its strategic backyard. In the case of Guatemala, military assistance was directed towards reinforcing the national intelligence apparatus and for training the officer corps in counterinsurgency techniques, key factors which had significant bearing on human rights violations during the armed confrontation.

Anti-communism and the National Security Doctrine (DSN) formed part of the anti-Soviet strategy of the United States in Latin America. In Guatemala, these were first expressed as anti-reformist, then anti-democratic policies, culminating in criminal counterinsurgency. The National Security Doctrine fell on fertile ground in Guatemala where anti-communist thinking had already taken root and from the 1930s, had merged with the defense of religion, tradition and conservative values, all of which were allegedly threatened by the world-wide expansion of atheistic communism. Until the 1950s, these views were strongly supported by the Catholic Church, which qualified as communist any position that contradicted its philosophy, thus contributing even further to division and confusion in Guatemalan society.

During the armed confrontation, the State's idea of the "internal enemy," intrinsic to the National Security Doctrine, became increasingly inclusive. At the same time, this doctrine became the *raison d'être* of Army and State policies for several decades. Through its investigation, the CEH discovered one of the most devastating effects of this policy: State forces and related paramilitary groups were responsible for 93% of the violations documented by the CEH, including 92% of the arbitrary executions and 91% of forced disappearances. Victims included men, women and children of all social strata: workers, professionals, church members, politicians, peasants, students and academics; in ethnic terms, the vast majority were Mayans....

COLLECTIVE ENEMY OF THE STATE

In the years when the confrontation deepened (1978-1983), as the guerrilla support base and area of action expanded, Mayans as a group in several different parts of the country were identified by the Army as guerrilla allies. Occasionally this was the result of the effective existence of support for the insurgent groups and of pre-insurrectional conditions in the country's interior. However, the CEH has ascertained that, in the majority of cases, the identification of Mayan communities with the insurgency was intentionally exaggerated by the State, which, based on traditional racist prejudices, used this identification to eliminate any present or future possibilities of the people providing help for, or joining, an insurgent project.

The consequence of this manipulation, extensively documented by the CEH, was massive and indiscriminate aggression directed against communities independent of their actual involvement in the guerrilla movement and with a clear indifference to their status as a non-combatant civilian population. The massacres, scorched earth operations, forced disappearances and executions of Mayan authorities, leaders and spiritual guides, were not only an attempt to destroy the social base of the guerrillas, but above all, to destroy the cultural values that ensured cohesion and collective action in Mayan communities....

DEVASTATION OF THE MAYAN PEOPLE

The Army's perception of Mayan communities as natural allies of the guerrillas contributed to increasing and aggravating the human rights violations perpetrated against them, demonstrating an aggressive racist component of extreme cruelty that led to the extermination *en masse,* of defenseless Mayan communities purportedly linked to the guerrillas — including children, women and the elderly — through methods whose cruelty has outraged the moral conscience of the civilized world.

These massacres and the so-called scorched earth operations, as planned by the State, resulted in the complete extermination of many Mayan communities, along with their homes, cattle, crops and other elements essential to survival. The CEH registered 626 massacres attributable to these forces.

The CEH has noted particularly serious cruelty in many acts committed by agents of the State, especially members of the Army, in their operations against Mayan communities. The counterinsurgency strategy not only led to violations of basic human rights, but also to the fact that these crimes were committed with particular cruelty, with massacres representing their archetypal form. In the majority of massacres there is evidence of multiple acts of savagery, which preceded, accompanied or occurred after the deaths of the victims. Acts such as the killing of defenseless children, often by beating them against walls or throwing them alive into pits where the corpses of adults were later thrown; the amputation of limbs; the impaling of victims; the killing of persons by covering them in petrol and burning them alive; the extraction, in the presence of others, of the viscera of victims who were still alive; the confinement of people who had been mortally tortured, in agony for days; the opening of the wombs of pregnant women, and other similarly atrocious acts, were not only actions of extreme cruelty against the victims, but also morally degraded the perpetrators and those who inspired, ordered or tolerated these actions.

During the armed confrontation the cultural rights of the Mayan people were also violated. The Army destroyed ceremonial centers, sacred places and cultural symbols. Language and dress, as well as other elements of cultural identification, were targets of repression. Through the militarization of the communities, the establishment of the Civil Patrols (PAC) and the military commissioners, the legitimate authority structure of the communities was broken; the use of their own norms and procedures to regulate social life and resolve conflicts was prevented; the exercise of Mayan spirituality and the Catholic religion was obstructed, prevented or repressed; the maintenance and development of the indigenous peoples' way of life and their system of social organization was upset. Displacement and refuge exacerbated the difficulties of practicing their own culture....

ACTS OF GENOCIDE

After studying four selected geographical regions, (Maya-Q'anjob'al and Maya-Chuj, in Barillas, Nentón and San Mateo Ixtatán in North Huehuetenango; Maya-Ixil, in Nebaj, Cotzal and Chajul, Quiché; Maya-K'iche' in Joyabaj, Zacualpa and Chiché Quiché; and Maya-Achi in Rabinal, Baja Verapaz) the CEH is able to confirm that between 1981 and 1983 the Army identified groups of the Mayan population as the internal enemy, considering them to be an actual or potential support base for the guerrillas, with respect to material sustenance, a source of recruits and a place to hide their members. In this way, the Army, inspired by the National Security Doctrine, defined a concept of internal enemy that went beyond guerrilla sympathizers, combatants or militants to include civilians from specific ethnic groups.

Considering the series of criminal acts and human rights violations which occurred in the regions and periods indicated and which were analyzed for the purpose of determining whether they constituted the crime of genocide, the CEH concludes that the reiteration of destructive acts, directed systematically against groups of the Mayan population, within which can be mentioned the elimination of leaders and criminal acts against minors who could not possibly have been military targets, demonstrates that the only common denominator for all the victims was the fact that they belonged to a specific ethnic group and makes it evident that these acts were committed "with intent to destroy, in whole or in part" these groups (Article II, first paragraph of the Convention)....

Faced with several options to combat the insurgency, the State chose the one that caused the greatest loss of human life among non-combatant civilians. Rejecting other options, such as a political effort to reach agreements with disaffected non-combatant civilians, moving of people away from the conflict areas, or the arrest of insurgents, the State opted for the annihilation of those they identified as their enemy.

In consequence, the CEH concludes that agents of the State of Guatemala, within the framework of counterinsurgency operations carried out between 1981 and 1983, committed acts of genocide against groups of Mayan people which lived in the four regions analyzed. This conclusion is based on the evidence that, in light of Article II of the Convention on the Prevention and Punishment of the Crime of Genocide, the killing of members of

Mayan groups occurred (Article II.a), serious bodily or mental harm was inflicted (Article II.b) and the group was deliberately subjected to living conditions calculated to bring about its physical destruction in whole or in part (Article II.c). The conclusion is also based on the evidence that all these acts were committed "with intent to destroy, in whole or in part" groups identified by their common ethnicity, by reason thereof, whatever the cause, motive or final objective of these acts may have been (Article II, first paragraph).

The CEH has information that similar acts occurred and were repeated in other regions inhabited by Mayan people....

In general, the State of Guatemala holds undeniable responsibility for human rights violations and infringements of international humanitarian law. The Chiefs of Staff for National Defense (Estado Mayor de la Defensa Nacional) was, within the Army, the highest authority responsible for these violations. Nevertheless, regardless of who occupied positions within this body, political responsibility rests with the successive governments. For this reason, the President of the Republic, as Commander in Chief of the Army and Minister of Defense, should be subject to the same criteria of responsibility, given that national objectives were prepared at the highest level of Government in accordance with the National Security Doctrine. Furthermore, it should also be taken into account that until 1986, nearly all the Presidents were high level members of the military, with specific knowledge of military structures and their procedures....

GUATEMALAN GENOCIDE: THE COUNTERPOINT

Steve Salisbury

Steve Salisbury is a regular correspondent for Jane's Intelligence Review *covering South and Central America.*

■ POINTS TO CONSIDER

1. Summarize the criticisms in this reading of the report by the Commission on Historical Clarification (CEH).

2. Discuss the troublesome aspects of registering anonymous accusations.

3. Why do critics of the CEH report question the U.S. role in genocide in Guatemala? What did U.S. President Bill Clinton say on his trip to Guatemala?

4. Describe the treatment of the guerrillas in the report. Does the report reflect a bias toward the guerrillas?

Steve Salisbury, "Guatemalan Human Rights Report Opens Old Wounds," **Jane's Intelligence Review,** 1 May 1999. Reprinted with permission, **Jane's.**

Right-wing activists cry foul at the magnitude of the vast disparity between state and guerrilla abuses registered by the CEH.

A historic report about human rights violations committed during the 36-year Guatemalan civil war was publicly released on 25 February [1999] in Guatemala City by the Commission for Historical Clarification (CEH). At the time, human rights workers, activists and some diplomats praised the report as a landmark for the advancement of human rights in Latin America and as a step toward clearing the way for national reconciliation. However, conservative sectors and others are expressing doubts about the Commission's claims of impartiality and its methodology, and say that some of its conclusions will only re-aggravate bitter social divisions.

ATROCITIES

The CEH registered a total of 42,275 victims, of which 23,671 were victims of arbitrary execution and 6,159 were forced disappearances. Pooling this data with information from other studies, the CEH estimates that the conflict produced at least 200,000 victims between 1962-96; some 83 percent of the identified victims were Mayan Indians and about 17 percent were Ladinos.

Yet the estimate of 200,000 victims is questioned. If this estimate were compared to the respective guerrilla and military tallies of their own dead, it would mean that there were about 66 civilians killed or physically harmed for every combatant killed.

The Guatemalan military officially acknowledges 1,893 troops killed during the entire war. A total of between 900 and 1,200 guerrilla combatants and militants had been killed, according to a tally of figures stated by a former guerrilla commander after the war. The CEH's count of 669 massacres (626 imputed to the state and 32 to the guerrillas) also raises questions. It averages to about one every 19 days over 34 years, which does not correspond with local press reports and official death notices. However, defenders of the report say these massacres happened in anonymity, were covered up and that the press could not report them for fear of reprisals and lack of means.

While right-wing activists say they could accept findings that government forces committed the majority of political killings and

Cartoon by Steve Sack. Reproduced by permission, **Star Tribune.**

other human rights abuses, they cry foul at the magnitude of the vast disparity between state and guerrilla abuses registered by the CEH. The massacre count is an example. Overall, the Commission blames government forces for 93 percent of human rights violations, attributing only three percent to the guerrillas. Conservatives say this could be a reflection of alleged political bias by the Commissioners — a German jurist and two Guatemalans. Their appointments were made in a process not open to the Guatemalan public.

ANONYMOUS EVIDENCE

Leaving aside the question of whether or not the Commissioners are biased, the decision by the CEH to register anonymous accusations plays a large part in the controversy. It was intended to protect witnesses, but it opens the door to charges that bogus, politically motivated accusations form part of the report. The role of the CEH was only to register testimonies, and not to prove or disprove their validity.

A former interior vice-minister, Mario Merida, claims that in some places complaints denouncing guerrilla abuses were not accepted by CEH personnel. "The response [of CEH workers in the provinces] always was, 'Here we only file complaints against the army,' " wrote Merida in Guatemala's *El Periodico* newspaper.

A specific case supporting Merida's statement comes from a coffee exporter. Says Alvaro Delgado: "The guerrillas had murdered one of our farm administrators, and we took this information to the Commission, but they refused to hear it."

On a geopolitical level, the CEH concludes that there was "political, logistic, instructional and training support provided by Cuba for the Guatemalan insurgents." Yet the CEH does not appear to single out the former U.S.S.R., despite research by independent scholars who have unearthed Soviet intelligence documents showing Soviet support for Central American revolutionaries *via* Cuba. The U.S., though, is singled out for its involvement in the conflict. The report blames the U.S. government for directly or indirectly abetting the Guatemalan state in carrying out some illegal operations.

U.S. COMPLICITY

Responding in local Guatemalan newspapers, U.S. Ambassador Donald Planty called this assertion an erroneous interpretation. "It was an armed conflict where the guilty are Guatemalans," he said. U.S. President Bill Clinton also had something to say. During his 10-11 March [1999] visit to Guatemala, he declared: "It is important that I state clearly that [U.S.] support for [Guatemalan] military forces or intelligence units which engaged in violent and widespread repression of the kind described in the report was wrong, and the United States must not repeat that mistake." He added: "This Commission report was a brave thing to do. The United States supports the peace process, including the effort to find the truth, even if it is not favorable to the United States. We contributed $1.5 million dollars (U.S.) to the work of the Commission; we declassified 4,000 documents at the request of the Commission. So, I basically support what you [Guatemalans] are trying to do, strongly."

President Clinton was walking a political and diplomatic tightrope. Having invested funds and support in the CEH report, the Clinton Administration would be hard-pressed to enter a debate about the report's shortcomings, faults and deficiencies. By admitting that the U.S. had made mistakes in Guatemala, President Clinton seemed to try to phrase his words in such a way so as not to give grounds to potential law suits for victims' compensation. Responding to Guatemalans' demands for this, President Clinton announced U.S. plans to seed economic development in the areas hit hardest by the war.

JUSTICE: A TALL ORDER

Retrospective justice in Guatemala is a tall order. The Guatemalan government has passed a general amnesty law to cover the combatants of the 36-year conflict. However, Article 8 of the Law of National Reconciliation clearly states that "crimes of genocide, torture, and forced disappearance, as well as those crimes...that do not admit extinguishment of penal responsibility of conformity with internal law or international treaties ratified by Guatemala" are not covered by the amnesty. This phrasing presents a Pandora's box of interpretations and could be legally used against amnesty defenses.

In the aftermath of the CEH report, human rights groups and activists on the left have demanded that active and retired military officers, former government authorities, large landowners and right-wing politicians implicated in war crimes be brought to justice. Their list is topped by former military heads of state General Romeo Lucas Garcia and General Efrain Rios Montt.

According to the CEH, the peak of state terror occurred in 1981 and 1982, during these strongmen's respective regimes. If there are no trials and punishment, says activist Juan Leon in *La Hora* newspaper, "any military person or civilian could commit terrifying acts against the people of Guatemala again." The report shows that the guerrillas also committed most of their atrocities in the early 1980s. However, many human rights and activist groups have remained silent about demands to bring to trial leaders of the former guerrilla group, the Guatemalan National Revolutionary Unit (URNG), which is now a legal political party. The CEH blames the URNG guerrilla high command for either ordering, instigating, allowing or condoning massacres and assassinations, including actions involving foreign nationals.

THE PINOCHET EFFECT

Will the U.S., Germany and other countries solicit the extradition of the killers of their diplomats and citizens? So far, there has been no news of extradition orders, though public pressure for extradition is growing, inspired by the legal case against former Chilean strongman Augusto Pinochet, who is detained under

MARXIST GUERRILLAS

Conservatives are not immune to mortal failings and temptations, including the failing of being inconsistent and the temptation to go easy on the enemy of one's enemy. If one regards armed Marxist insurgents as a dire threat to human life, liberty, and happiness, one is likely to make allowances for a government under siege by Marxist guerrillas....

Jeff Jacoby, "Double Standards, Left and Right," **Boston Globe,** 15 March 1999.

house arrest in the UK at the time of this writing. Reacting to demands for war crimes trials, the government and the URNG leadership have made apologies and asked for pardon.

It seems that the URNG may have thought it could use the human rights issue as a one-edged sword against the military. The military, which officially stood at 31,423 members on 29 March [1999] (down by about a third from its total strength of 46,900 personnel in 1997), may have believed that it could escape war crimes trials by turning human rights into a double-edged sword with which to slice the URNG. Now it appears that both the military and the URNG are shaken by the possibility that high-ranking members of each group may have to face costly legal entanglements.

President Alvaro Arzu, who has hitherto failed to denounce publicly General Romeo Lucas Garcia's human rights record, says he wants to take time to study the CEH's 3,600-page report before making detailed conclusions. However, his administration's initial position, shows that his government does not accept all the Commission's findings and recommendations. While the government says that it "acknowledges and values" the CEH's work, the government communique pointedly mentions "the complexity of the matter and its controversial character." The communique adds: "The government will take into account those aspects of the report that contribute to reconciliation."

MILITARY ABUSES

One aspect not being taken into account by the government is the CEH's recommendation that President Arzu create a new, independent commission to investigate the conduct of military officers during the war. The government says that there are already internal mechanisms for the "purging and professionalization of the security corps," and that the UN mission in Guatemala (MINUGUA) and other commissions are enough for verification.

However, Arzu has not shed any tears over the CEH's accusations against the Rios Montt regime. Rios Montt is the founder and driving force of the Guatemalan Republican Front political party (FRG), which is the strongest electoral and legislative opposition to Arzu's National Advancement Party (PAN). Opinion polls showed that Rios Montt would have beaten Arzu in the 1995 presidential election, had he not been constitutionally barred from the contest (and future presidential elections) for taking power as result of a coup in 1982.

As another presidential election approaches in the latter half of 1999 and PAN leads the FRG in volatile potential-voter surveys, Rios Montt dismisses human rights charges against him as politically inspired. The left-wing political alliance, including the URNG, trails far behind PAN and FRG. That, and the memory of Rios Montt's military success against the guerrillas (when he employed a "Beans and Rifles" strategy that fed and armed the peasantry) are what bother the left, says FRG legislator Aristides Crespo.

One of the stated purposes of the CEH's report is to promote reconciliation among Guatemalans, but with both the left and the right preparing for legal battle, it looks like Guatemala's recently ended war of bullets will become a war of court motions. Guatemala's population of some 11 million inhabitants, most of whom live in some degree of poverty, pray that this struggle does not once again take the form of political violence.

READING

12

CULTURAL GENOCIDE: CANADA'S STRUGGLE TO REPAIR THE PAST

Michael Downey

Michael Downey lives in Toronto, where he writes freelance for a number of newspapers and magazines in the United States and Canada. Although he covers a variety of subjects, he frequently writes on matters of humanity, history, science and health.

■ POINTS TO CONSIDER

1. Describe the "Sixties Scoop." Is genocide pertinent to a discussion about child removal policies?

2. Discuss the effects of Canada's policy of removing aboriginal children, according to the article.

3. Identify policy changes made in response to the child seizures. What is the response of aboriginal communities?

4. Evaluate the article's view of cross-cultural adoptions.

5. Explain the link between culture and genocide (see Reading Eight). Do you believe American and Canadian assimilation policies have been, historically, genocidal?

Michael Downey, "Canada's Genocide: Thousands Taken from Their Homes Need Help," **Maclean's,** 26 April 1999. Reprinted by permission, Michael Downey.

In the late '70s, Manitoba's native leaders rebelled against the permanent loss of their children.

Carla Williams was four when the authorities knocked on the door and took the terrified Manitoba native youngster away from her parents forever. It was 1968, and Williams was thrust into a white society where nobody spoke her native tongue. Three years of cultural confusion later, she was adopted by a family that then moved to Holland. There the young girl was permitted no contact with her grieving parents in Canada. Subjected to emotional and sexual abuse, she had three babies by the age of 16 — two of them, she says, by her adoptive father, and one was given up for adoption. Finally, after her descent into alcohol, drugs and prostitution,the Dutch government received an official request from Canada to have her returned. Williams left Amsterdam in 1989 at the age of 25, shouting, "I'm going home!" She returned to Canada too late to meet the parents she had barely known: after the removal of three of their children, her native mother and father committed suicide.

SIXTIES SCOOP

Williams, now a saleswoman in Winnipeg, has had considerable success in turning her life around. But a study sheds light on a tragically disruptive program that saw thousands of young natives removed from their families for three decades starting in the 1950s. Children from native communities in British Columbia, Alberta and Ontario as well as Manitoba were routinely shipped to non-native foster homes or adoptive families far from their homes. Most of the 3,000 from Manitoba alone and many from the other provinces went to the United States, where placement agencies often received fees in the $15,000 to $20,000 range from the adoptive parents. One Manitoba judge has branded the child seizures "cultural genocide," and they do seem to fall well within the United Nations post-Second World War definition of genocide, which includes "forcibly transferring children of [one] group to another group."

After almost a year of hearings, a report [was] delivered to the funding body, a joint committee of aboriginal groups and a unique partnership of four Ontario government ministries. Prepared by an aboriginal social agency, Native Child and Family Services of Toronto, and Toronto-based consultants Stevenato and Associates and Janet Budgell, the report examines the history of what authorities called the "apprehensions" of native children, which continued into the early 1980s. The practice is sometimes referred to as the Sixties Scoop because the numbers peaked during that decade.

The seizures were carried out by child welfare agencies that insisted they were acting in the children's best interest — simply moving them into a better environment than they were getting in their native parents' home. Forced apprehensions of native children in fact began up to five generations earlier with the creation of residential schools, which functioned more as alternative parenting institutions than educational facilities. Those strict boarding schools effectively incarcerated native children for ten months of the year.

Unfortunately, many of the students returned from residential schools as distant, angry aliens, lacking emotional bonds with their own families. Having missed out on nurturing family environments, they were ill-prepared to show affection or relate to their own children when they became parents — as most did at an early age. Then, in the 1950s and 1960s, the federal government delegated responsibility for First Nations health, welfare and educational services to the provinces, while retaining financial responsibility for natives. With guaranteed payments from Ottawa for each child apprehended, the number of First Nations children made wards of the state skyrocketed. In 1959, only one percent of Canadian children in custody were native; a decade later the number had risen to 40 percent, while aboriginals made up less than four percent of the population.

TERRIBLE CONSEQUENCES

Ultimately, it became clear that the seizures were doing terrible damage to uncounted numbers of young natives. "It was perhaps — perhaps — done with the best of intentions," says David Langtry, current assistant deputy minister of Manitoba's child and family services. "But once it became recognized that it was the wrong thing to do, changes were made to legislation." A process introduced in 1988, he says, assures that an aboriginal child removed from a family will be placed in a new home according to strict priorities, turning to a non-native placement only as a last resort.

As previous investigations in other provinces have shown, the Sixties Scoop adoptions were rarely successful and many ended with children committing suicide. The new Ontario report will undoubtedly refer to formal repatriation programs already in place in Manitoba and British Columbia — as well as Australia, where there was a similar seizure of aboriginals — with a view to helping others return to Canada, find their roots and locate their families. The study will also set the stage for new programs aimed at healing the collective native pain and perhaps, in time, the deep-rooted anger.

Individual stories of the Sixties Scoop paint a heart-wrenching picture. Sometimes, whole families of status and non-status Indian or Metis children were separated from each other, never to meet again. Names were changed, often several times. They were shipped thousands of kilometers from their people and denied contact with their parents, siblings or communities or information about their heritage or culture. Some were enslaved, abused and raped. And no Canadian body has ever officially taken responsibility, or apologized, for the policies.

The report [is] soft on blame but frank about the extent of the tragedy still gripping native parents and plaguing the thousands of survivors who lost their names, language, families, childhood and, above all, their identities. It will seek faster access to adoption records to speed repatriation. However, Sylvia Maracle, a member of the committee of the umbrella group that funded the study, says repatriations are only a partial remedy. "We need to bring them back into the native circle, she says, "in a way that is comfortable for them." The decision to commission the study recognized the bitterness felt by all native people, says Maracle, who is Mohawk. "We are grieving," she says, "we are angry and we must do something to at least start the healing and in a holistic way."

CULTURAL GENOCIDE

Joan Muir would agree. "I was taken away from my family because my grandparents were alcoholics," says the Vancouver resident, now 33, "and placed with adoptive parents who were — as social workers had noted on my records prior to adoption — known alcoholics and racists." Muir says she was raised to be ashamed of her native status. "It just hit me a couple of years ago, that it's OK not to hide it anymore," she says. "Now that I'm away from my adoptive parents, I'm allowed to be native."

The report [refers] to the tragic story of Richard Cardinal, a northern Alberta Metis forcibly removed from his family at age four. Over the next 13 years, he was placed in 28 homes and institutions. In one, he was beaten with a stick for wetting the bed. Another provided a bed just two feet wide in a flooded basement. One entire Christmas Day, while his adoptive family celebrated the holiday, Cardinal was kept outside in the cold, staring in. His suicide attempts began when he was nine. At his 16th foster home, aged 17, he nailed a board between two trees and hanged himself.

Toronto social worker Kenn Richard, a co-author of the report, says it outlines the history of the seizures through the words of people who experienced them firsthand. But he feels strongly that the practice was only one part of a long history of wrongheaded and disastrous policies towards Canada's native population. "It's the legacy of child welfare in this country," says Richard, "that we have dysfunctional families and a deep anger among aboriginals."

In the late '70s, Manitoba's native leaders rebelled against the permanent loss of their children. "This was cultural genocide," concluded Manitoba family court Judge Edwin Kimelman, called on to investigate the seizures in 1982. "You took a child from his or her specific culture and you placed him into a foreign culture without any [counselling] assistance to the family which had the child. There's something drastically and basically wrong with that." That year, Manitoba banned out-of-province adoptions of native children and overhauled its child welfare system. Native child welfare authorities were established across Canada.

HEALING

The task of repairing the damage is still under way. Lizabeth Hall, who grew up in a native family and now heads the B.C. repatriation program, was shocked at the loss of identity among those removed from their native community. "People have called and asked, 'Can you just tell me what kind of Indian I am?' " says Hall. "It made me cry. I'd like Canadians to know what happened and why. Non-natives always 'justify' their protection of natives; they don't realize the racism in that."

At a 1992 B.C. government hearing into the Sixties Scoop seizures, a First Nations elder addressed Canada's history of "protecting" aboriginals. "For 30 years," said the elder, "generations of our children, the very future of our communities, have been taken away from us. Will they come home as our leaders, knowing the power and tradition of their people? Or will they come home broken and in pain, not knowing who they are, looking for the family that died of a broken heart?" Those are questions that new repatriation and education programs could help answer.

READING

13

CULTURAL GENOCIDE: CANADA PUTS RACE BEFORE CHILDREN'S WELFARE

Deborah Jones

Deborah Jones is a freelance writer based in Vancouver, B.C.

■ POINTS TO CONSIDER

1. Describe the experience of the adopted woman in the article. What point is Jones trying to make by writing her story?

2. Explain the distinction between race, ethnicity, and culture, according to the article.

3. Compare and contrast Jones' view of the Sixties Scoop and other past policies with that of Downey (see Reading 12).

4. Does the author believe adoption laws redress crimes committed against aboriginals?

5. Summarize the argument for relaxing race/culture preferences in adoption.

Excerpted from Deborah Jones, "Canada's Real Adoption Crisis," **Chatelaine,** May 1998. Reprinted by permission of the author.

In the past, native kids were literally stolen from their parents because of their race; today, because of their race — and in a bizarre attempt to redress past wrongs — they may be denied adoption when they're taken into care.

Cecelia Reekie sometimes wonders how her life would have been different if she had not been adopted. She was born almost 35 years ago in Prince Rupert, B.C., to a 15-year-old white girl; her father was a 34-year-old native Canadian with a drinking problem. At six weeks of age, Reekie was taken in by a white family.

If you've read this far, you may already be thinking along a track we've become used to from reading so many sad stories. It goes something like this: adopted child becomes another statistic among native children whose absorption into white culture resulted in tragic misunderstanding, alienation, even abuse. Well, no. In fact, Reekie's is one of the happy adoption stories. Her adoptive parents and siblings welcomed her with love and treated her as an equal. Uncommonly for that era, they also raised her to be familiar with and proud of her native ancestry. There were tough times. But today Reekie is a successful adult with strong ties to both her birth and adoptive families.

THE LEGACY OF CULTURAL GENOCIDE

Unfortunately, positive stories like Reekie's are overwhelmed by the history of racism, cultural genocide and abuse of aboriginal children over many decades in Canada, and of rocky relations between other races. That legacy has become a labyrinth of rules, clearly legislated or unwritten and subtle, that form barriers to the adoption of Canadian children by parents of a different race.

In a perfect world, all the experts agree, all adopted children would be placed with terrific families that share their racial heritage. Trouble is, in Canada, untold thousands of children in care are nonwhite, and most families trying to adopt are Caucasian. There are many more white families wanting to adopt than there are white kids — and very long waiting lists. Consequently, hopeful parents are going to places like Haiti, China and Peru to adopt children who don't look like them anyway, while thousands of Canadian kids in care grow up in foster families, who ironically, are mostly Caucasian.

If Reekie had been born today, because of her father's native heritage, B.C. legislation would have likely prevented her adoption by nonnative parents. She might have been adopted by an aboriginal family, but more likely she would have ended up in a series of foster homes. Or she might have stayed with one or both of her birth parents. She muses, "What kind of a life would I have had? I don't think it would have been very good. I mean, my mom was 15 and my dad was a 34-year-old alcoholic."

RACE, CULTURE AND FOSTER CARE

It's a sad fact that lots of Canadian children— perhaps as many as 41,000 now in government care, according to one estimate — have birth families who can't, or won't, nurture them. The kids come in as many colors and shapes as they do cultural backgrounds. In a country that prides itself as multicultural, you'd think they'd all be cared for equally. They're not. In fact, race plays a big role in how lots of kids are raised.

In most activities in Canada, racism is banned outright. Deny someone a job, an education or a seat on a bus because of his or her skin color, and you can end up in court. Yet when it comes to adoption, decisions are commonly made on the basis of race, and in some cases they're legislated....

In this age of medical magic, should we scientifically investigate the genetic lineage of each child and place him or her with parents whose genes best match? Should we devise a point system that would account for skin pigmentation, hair and eye coloring, and cheekbone height, so that prospective parents could be evaluated depending on how well they physically match the child they want to adopt? Does this all sound ridiculous?

Unfortunately, it would be no more ridiculous than the haphazard way things were, and still are, done, especially with aboriginal children. In the past, native kids were literally stolen from their parents because of their race; today, because of their race — and in a bizarre attempt to redress past wrongs — they may be denied adopting when they're taken into care. There are no reliable numbers on children's ethnicity, but Viola Thomas, president of United Native Nations (an organization that works for the betterment of nonstatus off-reserve Canadian natives), estimates that about 40 to 70 percent of all children in government care, depending on the province and area, are aboriginal.

While the law doesn't ban transracial adoption, it certainly discourages it. Court rulings, legislation and tacit agreements comprise clear barriers to adoption by nonnative families. A friend of mine in Toronto was told by a social worker that he and his wife (both white) would not be eligible to adopt a black or native child. They were also urged to encourage any black or native families they knew to consider fostering or adopting because children desperately needed homes. In B.C., provincial legislation now requires social workers and courts to consider exposure to native culture as critical when considering what is in the best interest of any child with aboriginal heritage. In the end, children who would otherwise have permanent normative homes may be sentenced to a life of foster care....

If white parents adopt a minority child, [Professor Michael Sobol of the University of Guelph] says, "The family has to recognize that the child will be under assault. It takes a special kind of strong, intelligent and sensitive parent. At least if families look alike parents have usually had a shared experience, and the child has access to an extended family with the same cultural experience."

But research also shows that it's far better for kids to be adopted into a permanent transracial family than to be raised in the foster system as a ward of government. Transracial adoption under the right conditions can work....

TRANSRACIAL ADOPTION WORKS

"It wasn't always easy," Reekie says. "All kids go through a time, especially as teens, when they try and figure out who they are. Adoptees test the boundaries and push more because we've got it in our minds that we're disposable." But Reekie and her adoptive family survived the tumultuous teens. In her 20s, with the full support of her adoptive parents, Reekie sought out her birth parents. Her birth father, now a recovering alcoholic, had become hereditary chief of their Indian band and has a wife and family, while her birth mother, whose ancestry is French-Canadian, is also married. Through her father, Reekie became registered as a status Indian with Ottawa, and through his family she received her Indian name: New-Yam-Dzeets Aik-Sto-Kwia.

Now married with two children of her own, Reekie is in close contact with her birth and adoptive families, including parents, siblings and a wide network of relatives.

Is Cecelia Reekie's positive adoption tale the exception to the rule that adoption between races doesn't work? Reekie emphatically rejects the idea. "There are lots like me," she says with conviction....

The stories of Reekie show that with respectful, strong and inspired parenting transracial adoption can work. History, however, shows why this idea is so controversial.

For decades, Canadian governments essentially stole native children from their families. At first the kids were incarcerated in residential schools and returned to their homes during holidays. Later, in the 1950s and '60s, in a sort of free-for-all that native social workers and activists now call the Scoop, social workers apprehended aboriginal children and gave them to nonnative families to raise. Originally, perhaps, aboriginal children were taken to be educated and integrated. But in some residential schools, we've learned from well-publicized lawsuits and criminal convictions of staff, kids were placed in the care of pedophiles, zealots or abusive and neglectful caregivers and denied their culture....

Even efforts by well-meaning nonnative parents often failed with the children of the Scoop. While at the University of Calgary, Christopher Bagley studied 37 families who adopted aboriginal children and found that problems arose because aboriginal kids with nonnative parents still had to deal with discrimination yet lacked the strength they would have gained by positive exposure to their heritage....

LACK OF FOSTER HOMES

The race problem wouldn't exist if there were enough native families willing to take these kids in. But there aren't. Sheila Durnford of the British Columbia Federation of Foster Parent Associations, who has fostered six aboriginal children, says non-white children are currently trapped and are "falling through the cracks" because of lack of money for programs, social workers who are overworked and too few foster parents of aboriginal ancestry. Durnford agrees that black parents should care for black children and aboriginal children should stay in aboriginal families. "But it would be better for kids to be adopted by white families than to stay in foster care for the rest of their lives," she says....

Until more families from diverse ethnic groups become foster or adoptive parents, or until the social problems that dump so many thousands of children in government care are fixed, we should find ways to care for the thousands of children — ways that are not boxed in by race issues. As Cecelia Reekie says, "Adoption can't be a race issue. We as a society need to look after all our children, no matter what race they are."...

EXAMINING COUNTERPOINTS

This activity may be used as an individualized study guide for students in libraries and resource centers or as a discussion catalyst in small group and classroom discussions.

Former Chilean General Augusto Pinochet was arrested by British officials in London 17 October 1998 at the request of Spain. Spanish Magistrate Baltazar Garzon filed a petition with the British government asking for his extradition to Spain to face charges of genocide (broadening the definition to include the targeting of political opponents) and crimes against humanity, including torture and terrorism.

11 September 1973, General Pinochet led a military *coup d'etat* overthrowing Chile's democratically elected President, Salvador Allende. The U.S. is often blamed for destabilizing the country before the coup, as well as for assisting in the planning and implementation of the coup. Under Pinochet's 17-year-rule, the military government is accused of eliminating 3,000 political opponents and torturing thousands more, Spanish Nationals among them. General Pinochet negotiated the position of "Senator for Life" in the Constitution of Chile before he stepped down in 1990, ending military rule. The arrest of Pinochet spawned competing reactions in the international community. Many people have harshly criticized Tony Blair's government for honoring the request, while other nations have issued their own charges against the former dictator.

28 October 1998, the U.K. High Court declared Pinochet's detention unlawful. The court cited that his status as former head of state granted him immunity from arrest. That decision was overturned (3-2) on appeal by a panel of the British House of Lords 25 November. However, this ruling, too, was thrown out after advo-

cates for the General questioned the bias of a panel member, who was married to an Amnesty International advocate. A March 1999 ruling of a seven-member-panel affirmed the arrest but concluded that Pinochet could only be extradited to Spain and tried for crimes committed after 1988, the year the U.K. signed the Torture Convention.

The Point:

Pinochet is a perpetrator of genocide and torturer whose dictatorial rule ended for Chile what could have been "a third way" — a democratic transition to socialism. Had not the U.S. intervened to plan and support the bloody March 1973 coup, perhaps the lives of 3,000 people would have been spared, as well as the security and health of thousands more tortured by the military regime.

The Spanish Magistrate has established a profound principle — that dictators may not live comfortably with impunity after their crimes have been committed. The attempt to bring Pinochet to Spain to answer for his genocidal policies brings hope to human rights activists globally; for even though the Senator for Life could negotiate immunity in his nation, he will not be immune in the international community.

The Counterpoint:

The regime of Salvador Allende waged a war on private property that was devastating Chile's economy. Although elected democratically, Allende was the winner in a three-way election which neither gave him a majority of the vote nor any mandate to promote his Marxist-leaning policies. Surely headed for Communist revolution, as Chile became the new mecca for left wing terrorists from Cuba to East Germany, Pinochet prudently stepped in to save the nation from its impending doom. Today, with Pinochet largely to thank, Chile has a free market economy that is a model for the rest of Latin America.

The bizarre arrest of the General is an affront to the people of Chile and the principal of national sovereignty. His arrest and detention are extra-legal — not based upon law but upon assertions of "genocide" and "crimes against humanity" which exist in no nation's law books.

Guidelines:

For this study, conduct some brief research (i.e., through the worldwide web or through gathering past newspaper or magazine articles) before examining the point and counterpoint. Next examine the point and counterpoint and critique each view.

Questions:

1. Do you agree with the point or the counterpoint? Explain.

2. Are the events that occurred under Chilean military rule covered under The Genocide Convention? (See Reading Seven.)

3. Can you draw parallels among the topics in this book: the Holocaust, the decimation of Indigenous Americans, the Pol Pot regime, the Rwandan Genocide) and the military regime in Chile?

4. Do other nations have the right to prosecute leaders of sovereign states? (Consult Reading One.)

CHAPTER 3

CAMBODIA'S KILLING FIELDS: THE U.S., THE KHMER ROUGE AND GENOCIDE

INSIDE POL POT'S CAMBODIA, 1975-1979

John Barron

John Barron served as Senior Editor of Reader's Digest. *When he delivered his testimony in May 1977 before a U.S. House Subcommittee, Cambodia had been closed to the western media for over two years. Barron and his Southeast Asian Affairs Editor, Anthony Paul, relied on testimony from refugees who fled Cambodia after its capital Phnom Penh fell to the Khmer Rouge 17 April 1975. The Khmer Rouge, dominated by Pol Pot's high organization, ruled Cambodia until overthrown by the Vietnamese in 1979. Throughout this time Cambodia was largely a closed country.*

■ **POINTS TO CONSIDER**

1. According to Anthony Paul, what was daily life like in Cambodia under Khmer Rouge rule?

2. Describe the actions of the Khmer Rouge after occupying the capital city Phnom Penh.

3. What was Angka Loeu? What do Cambodians and outside observers know about Angka Loeu during the years of Khmer Rouge rule?

4. According to Barron, who were the targets of the new government?

Excerpted from the testimony of John Barron before the Subcommittee on International Organizations of the U.S. House Committee on International Relations, 3 May 1977.

As a consequence of this central rule by the Communist leaders who enshroud themselves under the title Angka Loeu, the people of Cambodia systematically are being denied virtually all human rights.

Between October 1975 and November 1976, we [Barron and Anthony Paul, Roving Editor] interviewed more than 300 Cambodian refugees, mainly in Thailand but also in Malaysia, France, and the United States. The men, women, and teenagers interviewed fled from different sections of Cambodia at different times during the 13 months of our initial research. They represented all socio-economic strata and all age groups, except the very young.

In March of 1977, Anthony Paul returned to the camps along the Thai-Cambodian border searching for recently arrived refugees with first-hand information about current conditions in Cambodia.

INSIDE POL POT'S CAMBODIA

He summarized the results of his interviews in a letter to me March 28.

Chantaburi, Thailand, March 28, 1977.

Dear John — I have just returned from a 1,200-kilometer swing through Thailand's camps for Cambodian refugees — at Aranyaprathet, Trad, Kamput and Laem Sing. I had expected some evidence of slackening terror in Cambodia. It is true that fewer refugees are escaping from that country into Thailand — the present rate is about 100 a month — but the stories they bring suggest that the killings have not yet stopped. Daily, acts of unspeakable barbarism continue to be perpetrated in the name of this once-gentle country's Communist revolution.

A crude but apparently effective system of spying operates in many villages. The Khmer Rouge often make a distinction between the former inhabitants of a village and the new arrivals, the so-called "people of the Emigration" (those Cambodians evacuated from cities, towns and villages and sent into the countryside in the days following the Communist victory). Long Ly, a 29-year-old former official of the Agriculture Ministry in Thmar Puok told me that the former inhabitants of his village were ordered by the Khmer Rouge to report on the newcomers. For thus cooperating with their Communist guards, these villager were given more rice than the displaced city-folk.

Anyone willing to inform on the emigrants finds ready listeners among the Khmer Rouge, whose paranoia appears to be boundless. Thirty-one-year-old Khao Thiem Ly is a former air traffic controller at Phnom Penh's Pochentong airport, who managed to conceal, until a day or so before last February, his service to the former government. The village to which he was "emigrated" in April 1975 was Prey Bhan village in the Chouk district, some 41 kilometers northwest of the port of Kampot by road. It is a small village — a population of about 360 at the moment — and of no particular importance. Yet, in the time he was there no fewer than 20 persons were executed for being "American spies," about five of these having been "uncovered" by Khmer Rouge late last year and early this year.

With some minor local variations, conditions at Prey Bhan were similar to all other villages from which refugees had recently escaped. The work schedule: rise at 5 a.m., work until 10:30 a.m. Begin work again at 12:30 p.m., work until 5:00 p.m. Further work on most nights, 7:00 p.m. to 9:00 or 10:00 p.m. No weekends or days off of any kind. One tin of rice per person per day until January, then slightly more following the introduction of a communal kitchen. Malaria and dysentery were rife — about ten people died of these diseases. Persons talking in groups of three or more; persons talking at night or moving at night from hut to hut or village to village; persons killing poultry without permission from Angka — all risked summary execution. Only former inhabitants of Prey Bhan were permitted near the communal kitchen without Angka's specific permission. The "emigrants" were allowed there only at their allotted meal times.

One of the most heinous crimes at Prey Bhan is to carry an affliction known to the Khmer Rouge as *khael chak*, literally "old scurf" or "old dandruff." This is the Cambodian revolutionary's metaphor for memories of other days — the car or

105

house or family left behind in Phnom Phenh, for example. The charge "You have old dandruff" is levelled at anyone who, for whatever reason, incurs the displeasure of the Communists. Says Khao, "A villager is given no more than two warnings about having 'old dandruff,' then he disappears."

To anyone familiar with what has been happening in Cambodia over the past couple of years, such stories, of course, are commonplace.

Immediately after the fall of Battambang in April 1975, Sek [Sa Moun] was one of thousands of people from that city sent to Svay Sor village, just outside of Krakor town. Shortly after he arrived, Khmer Rouge told the emigrants that the population of their newly constituted community was 12,750.

Almost from the beginning, Krakor's scanty food rations began to take their toll. Bodies weakened by malnutrition became increasingly susceptible to tropical diseases. The resultant death toll was swollen, of course, by the fairly constant stream of executions — or sudden disappearances — of Cambodians who had for whatever reason offended Angka Loeu, the Khmer Rouge "Organization on High."

Sek remembers that the worst period began late in the dry season of last year — about April or May. The rate of deaths by starvation and disease began picking up. "By June or July," says Sek, "about five people a day were dying. Sometimes in one day 20 to 30 people died of disease, their bodies swollen by malnutrition." The famine and plagues were accompanied by an increase in the rate of executions. Sek estimated that, from the end of the dry season to about November of last year, about 600 must have been eliminated. The program embraced soldiers, teachers, students and anyone who knew a foreign language. The Khmer Rouge were not reticent about letting the villagers see their victims. "We often found their bodies later," says Sek. "Usually their throats had been cut."

TONY
(ANTHONY M. PAUL),
Reader's Digest Roving Editor
(Asia and Pacific)

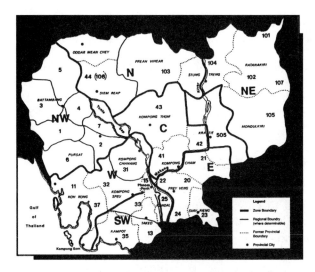

"Democratic Kampuchea," in Ben Kiernan, **The Pol Pot Regime: Race, Power and Genocide in Cambodia,** 1975-1979, New Haven: Yale University Press, 1996.

EMPTYING THE CITIES

Our accumulated data, I believe, conclusively demonstrate that the following has happened in Cambodia:

Within a few hours after occupying Phnom Pehn on April 17, 1975, the Communists, known among Cambodians as the Khmer Rouge, ordered the Capital evacuated. Within the next days, the entire population, estimated to have numbered at the time approximately three million, was expelled at gunpoint.

Soon other Cambodian cities, harboring all together approximately half a million people, were similarly evacuated. And later, probably another half million were driven from the larger villages to the territories controlled by the Government prior to April 17.

While draining the cities of all human life, the Khmer Rouge mounted a methodical assault on the physical symbols and sinews of preexisting Cambodian society and culture. Troops ransacked libraries, offices, and homes, burning books by the hundreds of thousands, along with written matter.

The purpose here, it seems to me, was to obliterate every vestige of Cambodian culture as it existed prior to April 1975.

Simultaneously, the Khmer Rouge commenced killing former military officers and civil servants of the Lon Nol government.

Thousands were slaughtered in organized massacres conducted outside the cities according to the same basic pattern.

Officers and senior civil servants who managed initially to conceal their past identity were killed whenever and wherever unmasked. In a number of cases described by eye witnesses, their families, including children and infants, were killed along with them.

HIGH ORGANIZATION

Now, some of these exiles were fortunate enough to be consigned to new settlements relatively close to the cities and thus, for them, the ordeal of the march lasted relatively a short time. Hundreds of thousands, if not millions, of others marched for weeks, goaded ever onward into the countryside without knowing what their ultimate destination or fate would be.

The eventual destination of most was a new settlement. Thousands of these new settlements were hewn out of the bush, scrubland, and jungle. Typically, upon arriving, a new villager family would be ordered to construct a hut out of bamboo leaves, whatever could be foraged from the jungle, and then were put into a work group normally comprised of ten families.

The work groups labored and still do labor from 5:00 or 6:00 a.m. in the morning to the midday break and then until 5:00 or 6:00 p.m. at night. On moonlit nights, in many areas work continued from 7:00 to 10:00 p.m. And this all goes on seven days a week.

There were in many areas a lack of agricultural implements, tools, so much of the work had to be done by hand by people who were unaccustomed to arduous physical labor.

Every phase of life was soon strictly regimented according to dictates from Angka Loeu, the High Organization or Organization on High, in whose name Cambodia has been ruled since the Communist conquest.

Generally, anyone violating the strictures of Angka or thought to be violating them received a warning known as a "kosang." A second transgression brought a second warning. A third transgression resulted in execution or "disappearance," which was widely believed — and, I believe, correctly — to be the same as execution. However, anyone caught trying to escape usually was shot without warning.

By late summer of 1975, food shortages reached famine level in large portions of the country. Epidemics of cholera, malaria, and dysentery incapacitated a sizable percentage of the new villagers. Given the demanding work regimen, the tropical squalor, and the almost total lack of modern medicine, the death rate inevitably was high in the settlements.

In the autumn of 1975, Angka Loeu ordered field commanders to prepare for the extermination, after the forthcoming harvest, of all former government soldiers and civil servants, regardless of rank, and their families.

PURGES

Soon word spread among Communist soldiers that former teachers, village chiefs, and students also were to be massacred. The second organized slaughter began early in 1976. Now the lowliest private, the most humble civil servant, and most innocent teachers, even foresters and public health officials, became prey.

The testimony of one Cambodian physician indicates that some intellectuals after servitude in the fields or incarceration in prison were concentrated in special villages for reeducation. However, the physician's own experiences, as well as accounts of numerous other refugees, indicates that many teachers, students, and educated people were killed simply because of their class or education.

However, the evacuation of the cities, the methodical assault upon symbols of the past, the carefully organized massacres in different parts of the country, the establishment of thousands of new villages, the imposition of more or less uniform work patterns, modes of behavior, and discipline, clearly reflect systematic central planning and direction.

As a consequence of this central rule by the Communist leaders who enshroud themselves under the title Angka Loeu, the people of Cambodia systematically are being denied virtually all human rights.

READING

15

KILLING BIRDS: THE U.S. AND CAMBODIA, 1969-1973

Ben Kiernan

Ben Kiernan is Associate Professor of History and Director of the Cambodian Genocide Program at Yale University.

■ **POINTS TO CONSIDER**

1. Describe the factions within the Communist party in Cambodia.

2. Examine U.S. actions toward Cambodia. Were these actions consistent with policy?

3. Evaluate the effects of U.S. escalation of the Vietnam War, according to Kiernan.

4. Discuss Kiernan's statement, "Pol Pot's revolution would not have won power without U.S. economic and military destablization of Cambodia."

Excerpted from Ben Kiernan, **The Pol Pot Regime: Race, Power, and Genocide in Cambodia under the Khmer Rouge,** 1975-79, New Haven: Yale University Press, 1996. Copyright © 1996, Yale University Press. Reprinted with permission, Yale University Press.

Pol Pot's revolution would not have won power without U.S. economic and military destablization of Cambodia. This was probably the most important single factor in Pol Pot's rise.

In 1954 the Cambodian Communist party had been largely rural, Buddhist, moderate, and pro-Vietnamese. By 1970 its leadership was urban, French-educated, radical, and anti-Vietnamese. A major factor in this "changing of the vanguard" was the rivalry between Chinese and Vietnamese Communists for influence in this part of Southeast Asia. While China supported [Cambodia's Prince] Sihanouk, it also encouraged a formerly pro-Vietnamese Communist movement whose new leaders were preparing to distance themselves from Hanoi. Thus Beijing's sponsorship provided Pol Pot's faction with manueverability that it would not otherwise have enjoyed....

U.S. INTERVENTION

Although it was indigenous, Pol Pot's revolution would not have won power without U.S. economic and military destabilization of Cambodia, which began in 1966 after the American escalation in next-door Vietnam and peaked in 1969-73 with the carpet bombing of Cambodia's countryside by American B-52s. This was probably the most important single factor in Pol Pot's rise....

Prince Sihanouk's Cambodia depended for its revenue on taxing rice exports. It now plunged towards bankruptcy. In December 1965, U.S. intelligence noted that Sihanouk was already complaining privately about "considerable loss of revenue" as a result of "the illicit traffic in rice from Cambodia to Vietnam."[1] Over the next year, taxable rice exports fell by two-thirds, from 490,000 tons in 1965 to only 170,000 in 1966. (Later figures are not available.) About 130,000 tons of rice, 40 percent of rice exports for 1966,[2] were smuggled to Vietnamese Communist agents and to black market circles in Saigon.

Equally important, the Vietnamese Communists were resorting increasingly to the use of Cambodian territory for sanctuary from American attack. By the end of 1965, according to the U.S. intelligence report, they had established "clandestine and probably temporary facilities" there, but that year had already seen "eight instances of fire fights between Cambodian border forces and the

Viet Cong." And U.S. aircraft in hot pursuit bombed and strafed Cambodia's border areas. Sihanouk's government claimed in 1966 that "hundreds of our people" had already died in American attacks.[3]

The U.S. intervention in Vietnam also produced a wave of Khmer refugees. From the early 1960s, Khmer Krom [ethnically Khmer, living in South Vietnam] began fleeing to Cambodia to escape the Saigon government's repression in the countryside. In 1962 a Khmer Buddhist monk who had fled the Diem regime with four hundred others claimed: "Our schools have all been closed...With the slaughter of our people, the destruction of our villages, the repression of our culture and language, it seems our people are to be exterminated." Between 1965-68, over 17,000 Khmers, including over 2,300 Buddhist monks, fled South Vietnam for Cambodia.[4]

Since the early 1960s, U.S. Special Forces teams, too, had been making secret reconnaissance and mine-laying incursions into Cambodian territory. In 1967 and 1968, in Operation Salem House, about eight hundred such missions were mounted, usually by several American personnel and up to ten local mercenaries, in most cases dressed as Viet Cong. One Green Beret team "inadvertently blew up a Cambodian civilian bus, causing heavy casualties." The code name of the operation was changed to Daniel Boone, and from early 1969, the number of these secret missions doubled. By the time of the 18 March 1970 coup against Sihanouk, over a thousand more had been mounted. In a total of 1,835 missions, twenty-four prisoners were taken, and an unknown number of people were killed or wounded by the "sanitized self-destruct antipersonnel" mines that Daniel Boone teams were authorized to lay up to thirty kilometers inside Cambodia.[5]...

SIHANOUK OVERTHROWN

Starting exactly a year before the coup [which overthrew Prince Sihanouk and installed Lon Nol] (on 18 March 1969), over 3,600 secret B-52 raids were also conducted over Cambodian territory. These were codenamed Menu; the various target areas were labeled Breakfast, Snack, Lunch, Dinner, Dessert, and Supper.[6] About 10,000 tons of bombs were dropped; the civilian toll is unknown. The U.S. aim was to destroy Vietnamese Communist forces in Cambodia or drive them back into Vietnam. But in September 1969, Lon Nol reported an increase in the number of

Communist troops in the sanctuaries, an increase that he said was partly motivated by "the cleaning-up operation" of the U.S.-Saigon forces. He added ominously, "In this period, nothing suggests that these foreign units will soon leave our territory.[7] Like the failing economy, this was one of the major factors in Sihanouk's downfall at Lon Nol's hands. Both factors were exacerbated by the U.S. escalation of the Vietnam War.

By 1970 Cambodia's frontier with Vietnam was breaking down. It was unable to withstand the pressure exerted by the two mighty contending forces that had been expanding and straining against one another in the limited space of southern Vietnam since the escalation of 1965. The pressure was economic, demographic, political, and military. Cambodia's rice crop drained into devastated Vietnam, while both Khmers and Vietnamese fled into Cambodia, with the U.S. military and air force in pursuit.

Richard Nixon's May 1970 invasion of Cambodia (undertaken without informing Lon Nol's new government) followed simultaneous invasions by Saigon and Vietnamese Communist forces. It created 130,000 new Khmer refugees, according to the Pentagon.[8] By 1971, 60 percent of refugees surveyed in Cambodia's towns gave U.S. bombing as the main cause of their displacement.[9] The U.S. bombardment of the Cambodian countryside continued until 1973, when Congress imposed a halt. Nearly half of the 540,000 tons of bombs were dropped in the last six months.[10]

From the ashes of rural Cambodia arose Pol Pot's Communist Party of Kampuchea (CPK). It used the bombing's devastation and massacre of civilians as recruitment propaganda and as an excuse for its brutal, radical policies and its purge of moderate Communists and Sihanoukists.[11] This is clear from contemporary U.S. government documents and from interviews in Cambodia with peasant survivors of the bombing....

INTENSIFIED BOMBING CAMPAIGN

In 1973 the United States withdrew its troops from Vietnam and trained its air force on Cambodia. The Secretary of the Air Force later said that Nixon "wanted to send a hundred more B-52s. This was appalling. You couldn't even figure out where you were going to put them all."[12]...

In March 1973 the bombardment spread west to envelop the whole country. Around Phnom Penh, 3,000 civilians were killed

FEEDING AN ARMY

Had the United States and China allowed it, Cambodia's suffering could have stopped when the Vietnamese finally responded to years of Khmer Rouge attacks across their border and liberated the country in January 1979. But almost immediately the United States began secretly backing Pol Pot in exile....

If on his deathbed Pol Pot had felt moved to offer thanks to his Western collaborators, he surely would have made special mention of an unworkable UN "peace plan" imposed by the West and China in 1992. At the insistence of Washington and Beijing, the Khmer Rouge was included in the UN operation as a legitimate "warring faction."...In 1993 the UN's military maps showed that in half of Cambodia Pol Pot had a military advantage he did not have before the UN arrived....

John Pilger, "The Friends of Pol Pot," **The Nation,** 11 May 1998.

in three weeks. At the time *UPI* reported: "Refugees swarming into the Capital from target areas report dozens of villages...have been destroyed and as much as half their population killed or maimed in the current bombing raids."[13]

Days later, the U.S. bombardment intensified, reaching a level of 3,600 tons per day.[14] As William Shawcross reported in *Sideshow,* the "wholesale carnage" shocked the chief of the political section in the U.S. embassy, William Harben....

But in July and August 1973 the Southwest Zone of Cambodia was carpet-bombed. It was the most intensive B-52 campaign yet. Its impact in the Southwest was not simply to destroy many more civilian lives. Politically, it tipped what had been a delicate CPK factional balance there[15] in favor of Pol Pot's "Center."...

Another report to the U.S. Army in July 1973 stated that "the civilian population fears U.S. air attacks far more than they do Communist rocket attacks or scorched-earth tactics."[16] Up to 150,000 civilian deaths resulted from the U.S. bombing campaigns in Cambodia from 1969 to 1973....

WINNING FACTION

In 1974, [then U.S. Secretary of State Henry] Kissinger was unsure if the Cambodian insurgency was "regional" and "factionalized" with only "a veneer of central control" or whether "the real power" lay with Pol Pot's Center.[17] The tragedy is that the former had been largely true in 1972, the latter was largely true in 1974, and Kissinger and Nixon were largely responsible for the change. Attempts on their part to rewrite the record are not surprising.

Communist Party cadres told young peasant victims of the bombing that "the killing birds" had come "from Phnom Penh" (not Guam), and that Phnom Penh must pay for its assault on rural Cambodia.[18] On the day the bombing ended, CPK propaganda leaflets found in bomb craters attacked the "Phnom Penh warriors" who were, they vowed, soon to be defeated.[19] The popular outrage over the U.S. bombing, predictably manipulated by the CPK, was as fatal for the two million inhabitants of Phnom Penh as it was for moderate Khmer Rouge and for Lon Nol's regime....

NOTES FOR READING FIFTEEN

1 Ben Kiernan, *How Pol Pot Came to Power,* London: Verso, 1985, p. 228,

2 Rémy Prud'homme, *L'Economie du Cambridge,* Paris, 1969, p. 255, table 12, note a.

3 Kiernan. *How Pol Pot,* pp. 228-9, 285.

4 Ben Kiernan, "Put Not Thy Trust in Princes: Burchett on Kampuchea," in Kiernan, ed., *Burchett: Reporting the Other Side of the World,* 1939-1983, London: Quartet, 1986, pp. 252-69.

5 W. Shawcross, Sideshow: *Kissinger, Nixon and the Destruction of Cambodia,* London: Deutsch, 1979, pp. 65, 24; S. Hersh, *The Price of Power: Henry Kissinger in the Nixon White House,* New York: Summit Books, 1983, pp. 177-8.

6 Shawcross, *Sideshow,* p. 27.

7 Kiernan, *How Pol Pot,* p. 286.

8 Hersh, *The Price of Power,* p. 202.

9 G.C. Hildebrand and G. Porter, *Cambodia: Starvation and Revolution,* New York: Monthly Review Press, 1976, p. 109, n. 83.

10 Ben Kiernan, "The American Bombardment of Kampuchea, 1969-1973" *Vietnam Generation,* vol. 1, no. 1, Winter 1989, pp. 4-41.

11 Kate G. Frieson, *The Impact of Revolution on Cambodian Peasants,* 1970-1775, Ph.D. diss., Dept. of Politics, Monash University, Australia, 1991, p. 188.

12 Shawcross, *Sideshow,* pp. 218-9.

13 United Press International Dispatch, Boston, 1 April 1973, Emphasis added.

14 Dana Adams Schmidt, *Christian Science Monitor,* 5 April 1973.

15 Kiernan, *How Pol Pot,* ch. 8.

16 "Effectiveness of U.S. Bombing in Cambodia," U.S. Army document dated 21 August 1973, p. 2.

17 "Emergence of Khmer Insurgent Leader Khieu Samphan on the International Scene," cable from Secretary of State to U.S. Embassy, Phnom Penh, April 1974.

18 Staffan Hildebrand, personal communication.

19 U.S. Army, Intelligence Information Report," Bomb Damage Assessment, Cambodia," no. 2725 1716 73, 22 August 1973, p. 2.

READING

16

POL POT'S DEATH AND HIS PLACE IN HISTORY

Jeffrey Hart

Jeffrey Hart is a distinguished Professor of English at Dartmouth College. The following reading, excerpted from Hart's twice-weekly syndicated column, is a reflection on Pol Pot on occasion of his death 15 April 1998.

■ **POINTS TO CONSIDER**

1. Identify the paradigm the author constructs.

2. What was the motivation of Pol Pot and other "similar dictators," in Hart's estimation?

3. Summarize the criteria for "murderous master spirits." How do these dictators differ from "lesser authoritarian figures"?

4. Describe Pol Pot's role in the 20th century, according to Hart. Keeping in mind that 1.5 million people died in Pol Pot's regime, do you agree with his assessment?

Excerpted from Jeffrey Hart, "Pol Pot Was a Child of His Century," **Conservative Chronicle,** 6 May 1998: 24. Reprinted with permission, King Feature Syndicate.

Let us hope that the world has learned a lesson about building new societies on the basis of a theory.

Pol Pot represented a political phenomenon that might well be the special signature of the 20th century. In that sense, he was not some sort of a demon or madman, but a child of his century.

CHILD OF HIS CENTURY

When Pol Pot was consigning a million of his Cambodian countrymen to the killing fields, slaughtering almost 15 percent of the country's population, he was outdoing on a per-capita basis both Mao Tse-tung and Josef Stalin. Those two, according to best estimates, killed some 70 million between them but had far more people at their disposal than did Pol Pot.

Ho Chi Minh, another Communist visionary who has been sentimentalized, belongs with them on a smaller scale, as do Fidel Castro and Che Guevara. Ho's vision cost an estimated two million lives, including some 300,000 who chose the South China Sea on rafts rather than his "new society."

Alongside Mao and Stalin, Adolf Hitler is a piker. He killed some six million Jews, and perhaps three million others, on a theory that they were biologically or politically unassimilable to his vision of the new Third Reich.

REMAKING SOCIETY

Each of the major 20th century despots wanted to remake society, and they could mobilize the full power of the state to test their theory.

So now Pol Pot, who supposedly died of natural causes, has been hurriedly cremated on a crude pyre of branches and weeds, with some remaining fighters from his Khmer Rouge tossing gasoline on the fire to make it burn hotter.

There is much talk about it being too bad that he was not brought to justice before some sort of international tribunal. But what would such a trial have accomplished? His crimes have been documented already. There is no further "record" to make there. What sort of trial would have been appropriate for Hitler, Stalin or Mao? Their record was clear. No punishment would have been appropriate for their crimes. Although they evaded

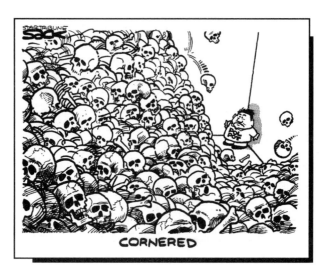

Cartoon by Steve Sack. Reproduced by permission, **Star Tribune.**

some sort of "court" by dying, they cannot evade the court of civilized history.

Only a few dictators reach the status of a Mao or Hitler. The century also has had its share of more ordinary authoritarian figures such as Francisco Franco, Benito Mussolini, Antonio Salazar and Augusto Pinochet. Such dictatorial figures usually emerge in response to a local crisis. Unlike the major dictators, they characteristically distrust theory and have limited ambitions.

The 20th century's murderous master spirits were men of vision, men with a theory about how to build a new society — which always means destroying the old one. And they were men of intellect.

SHAPING HISTORY

The historian John Gray of the London School of Economics wrote well about the subject in a recent review of James C. Scott's new study, "Seeing Like a State."

"The 20th century has seen many grand schemes for improving the human condition," Gray wrote. "These bold experiments had one thing in common: All failed."

Probably they all were driven by disgust. One can understand the disgust of Mao or Pol Pot at the intractable peasant societies

TRIUMPH OF THE PROLETARIAT

I might have hoped that, after Hitler, the world would have finally learned its lesson on genocide, and that holocausts would have been something of the past. Obviously, it hasn't. In its own way, the indifference of the world to the events in Cambodia is almost as appalling as what has happened there itself.

It almost seems to me that there is a kind of implicit racism in our response, in the sense that they are not whites or Jews or Westerners who are being murdered, but Orientals. Perhaps to us, Oriental life isn't worth as much as Western life.

This is a relatively unpredecented historic event. Here is a revolutionary regime presumably imbued with Marxist ideology. Marx talked about the triumph of the proletariat, not the elimination of the proletariat. Even the Chinese, who came to power on the basis of what was essentially an agrarian revolution, made no effort to completely depopulate their cities and transfer the urban population to the countryside.

I wonder if you have any sense of the kind of ideological justification for what has happened in Cambodia, as presented by the leaders of Democratic Kampuchea — what they hope to accomplish — what led to the development of the kind of ideology which led them to embark on what I think is a virtually unprecedented effort to completely uproot the social and economic bases of their society, to embark on a systematic slaughter of an inordinately high percentage of their own people?

I have no doubt that the dropping of 500,000 tons of bombs may have enraged them, but we dropped infinitely more tonnage on Vietnam and, whatever the situation may be there, I don't know that they are systematically destroying their own people.

There are plenty of other countries that have suffered grievously in war which, when a new government came to power, didn't embark on what has been going on in Cambodia.

Excerpted from the testimony of Congressperson Stephen J. Solarz before the Subcommittee on International Organizations of the U.S. House Committee on International Relations, 3 May 1977.

they grew up in, and disgust at colonial overlords. Out of their disgust came, no doubt, an overpowering desire to start from scratch, to repeal history.

One can understand the fanaticism of Ho Chi Minh or Fidel Castro as a reaction against perceived and seemingly intractable conditions. What is difficult to understand is their ruthless willingness to sacrifice any number of lives to bring about their vision.

In John Gray's famous line, they were willing to wade through slaughter to a throne. And, as John Gray says, their visions have all come to nothing, or much worse than nothing.

It is worth noting that almost all the century's mass killers had at one time or another the admiration, often enthusiastic, of the intellectual and academic classes.

Hitler, by and large, did not have such admirers in the democracies. But he, too, was a man of sweeping theory.

Hitler's vision of a new society was a bit different. Disgusted by the defeat of Germany in World War I, he apparently believed that a more biologically pure Reich would win the next war.

The United States under President Franklin D. Roosevelt backed Winston Churchill's England — illegally often. Then he orchestrated a contradictory alliance with Stalin to defeat Hitler.

Later, in a vast geopolitical maneuver, Roosevelt's successors used a reinvigorated Europe plus American economic and military power to win the Cold War and finish off the Soviet Union.

In the history of the 20th century, such figures as Pol Pot were relatively minor players, because their fields of action were relatively limited. And their countries undoubtedly will recover.

Let us hope that the world has learned a lesson about building new societies on the basis of a theory, and that the acrid smoke of the burning wood and gasoline from Pol Pot's pyre will be a symbolic end of it all as the 20th century nears its violent end.

READING

17

POL POT'S DEATH AND HIS PLACE IN MEDIA

Edward S. Herman

Edward S. Herman is Professor Emeritus of Finance at the Wharton School, University of Pennsylvania. He is the author of numerous books on economics, the media, and foreign policy including Manufacturing Consent: The Political Economy of the Mass Media, *with Noam Chomsky. Also in press is* The Myth of the Liberal Media: An Edward Herman Reader, *edited by Peter Lang, 1999.*

■ POINTS TO CONSIDER

1. Summarize the problems with the coverage of genocide in Cambodia.

2. According to Herman, how did the U.S. use Pol Pot to "punish" Vietnam?

3. Evaluate the pertinence of Suharto and Indonesia to this article.

4. Compare and contrast the media coverage of Cambodia and Indonesia.

5. How does the author feel about the communist-capitalist paradigm? Contrast this view with the view of the previous reading.

Excerpted from Edward S. Herman, "Pol Pot's Death in the Propaganda System," **Z Magazine,** June 1998. Reprinted by permission of the author.

***No longer useful in punishing Vietnam, and with no
economic interests anxious to protect his image (as
with Indonesia's [former] president Suharto), Pol Pot
has resumed his role as an object lesson in the
dangers of Communism and attempts to create a
"utopia of equality."***

The death of Pol Pot on April 15, 1998, unleashed a media
barrage of indignation and sanitized history that illustrates well
their role as agents in a system of propaganda. While Pol Pot was
undoubtedly a mass killer and evil force, and deserves angry condemnation, the U.S. media's indignation ebbs and flows in accord
with the demands of U.S. foreign policy. In the cases of both Pol
Pot and Saddam Hussein, periods of U.S. support of these criminals were accompanied by virtual silence on their misbehavior,
whereas in times of official hostility the media have shifted to furi-
ous but hypocritical indignation, along with carefully modulated
history. Today, no longer useful in punishing Vietnam, and with
no economic interests anxious to protect his image (as with
Indonesia's [former] president (Suharto), Pol Pot has resumed his
role as an object lesson in the dangers of Communism and
attempts to create a "utopia of equality."

DECADE OF GENOCIDE

There are, however, three problems that the media have had to
confront in assailing Pol Pot for committing genocide in
Cambodia. One is that the Cambodian genocide — a "decade of
genocide" according to a Finnish government research inquiry —
had two phases, in the first of which — 1969-1975 — the U.S.
was the genocidist. In that period, the U.S. Air Force dropped over
500,000 tons of bombs on rural Cambodia, killing scores of thousands, creating a huge refugee population, and radicalizing the
countryside. The number of U.S.-caused deaths in the first phase
is comparable to, or greater than, CIA and other serious estimates
of Pol Pot killings by execution (50,000-400,000). Cambodia
experts like Milton Osborne and David Chandler have contended
that the devastation hardened Khmer Rouge attitudes and made
for vengeful and violent behavior. Furthermore, when the Khmer
Rouge took over in April 1975, the country was shattered, starvation and disease were already rampant — 8,000 people a day
were dying in Phnom Penh alone — and these residual effects of
phase one were certain to take a toll in the years to follow. In

short, focusing solely on Pol Pot and making the U.S. an innocent bystander in the Cambodian genocide requires well-constructed blinders.

PUNISHING VIETNAM

A second problem for the media is that following the ouster of Pol Pot by the Vietnamese in December 1978, Pol Pot's forces found a safe haven in Thailand, a U.S. client state, and for the next 15 years or more were aided and protected there by Thai, Chinese, British, and U.S. authorities. The U.S. backed Pol Pot's retention of Cambodia's seat in the UN after his ouster (which was greeted with outrage in the West and was the grounds for intensified economic and political warfare against Vietnam). This support was designed to hurt Vietnam, which had occupied Cambodia and installed the friendly Hun Sen government in place of Pol Pot. When Vietnam sought a settlement in the late 1980s, the U.S. insisted strenuously that Pol Pot be included in the "peace process" with "the same rights, freedoms and opportunities" as any other party. In anticipation of a settlement, in the early 1990s the U.S. and its allies not only protected Pol Pot's forces from defeat by the Cambodian army, they helped him rebuild his strength and standing. During this period, the U.S. (and UN) refused to allow the Pol Pot regime to be referred to as genocidal. In order to oust the Vietnam-supported government, the U.S. strove to preserve Pol Pot and make him a significant force in the political struggle in Cambodia.

It is obvious that its long, active support of Pol Pot, as well as its role in the first phase of the genocide, makes the U.S. sponsorship of a Cambodia Documentation Center to assemble evidence solely on Pol Pot's crimes, and its recent alleged interest in bringing him to trial, dishonest, hypocritical, and problematic. Wasn't the U.S. support from 1979-1995 legitimizing? Isn't the U.S. implicated in his numerous crimes in cross-border raids, 1979-1998, which killed large numbers of Cambodians?

DOUBLE STANDARD

A third problem for the media is the biased selectivity in the choice of villain and of victims worthy of (crocodile) tears. The obvious comparison, and the one I will explore here, is with Suharto. Suharto came to power in 1965 accompanied by a slaughter of over 700,000 people. This was cold-blooded killing, designed to wipe out a mass movement that was seen as a political threat, without even a vengeance motive. Suharto also invaded East Timor in 1975, and over the years was responsible for the death of perhaps 200,000 of a population of some 700,000. So Suharto was guilty not only of a huge internal slaughter comparable in scale to that of Pol Pot, he also engineered a genocide in a neighboring country.

But of course all Suharto's killing was done with the approval and active support, or acquiescence, of the U.S. government and the West in general. In the case of the internal genocidal effort of 1965-66, the U.S. had already armed and trained the Indonesian military, urged it to act, gave Suharto and his associates lists of people to be killed, and both in private and public exulted in the outcome. He destroyed not only a Communist party, but the only mass-based political organization in the country, one that "had won widespread support not as a revolutionary party but as an organization defending the interests of the poor within the existing system" (Harold Crouch, *Army and Politics in Indonesia).* The U.S. has never liked mass-based political parties that work in the interests of the poor, whether in Vietnam, Indonesia, Guatemala, or Nicaragua....

In contrast with those pursuing [the interests of the poor] or a "utopia of equality," Suharto engaged in a class cleansing by mass murder, and then offered an "open door utopia for investors" — and a looting utopia for himself, his family, and his cronies. It follows from the difference in utopian objective that his victims were not "worthy," and that he is a statesperson rather than a villain in the eyes of the Western establishment. But this rests on a blatant elite and immoral double standard, reproduced in the mainstream media.

INTO THE BLACK HOLE

In discussing Pol Pot's recent death and villainy, how did the mainstream media handle the problem of the first phase of the Cambodian genocide in which the U.S. killed vast numbers and left a devastated country? The answer is: by a virtually complete blackout. Aside from a reference by Peter Jennings on "ABC News" to the "unpleasant" fact that our bombing had helped bring Pol Pot to power, I did not find a single editorial or news reference to the first phase: for the media, Cambodia's problems started in April 1975, and all deaths from starvation and disease, as well as executions, are allocated entirely to Pol Pot and his Communist utopian fanaticism. In the *New York Times,* the Khmer Rouge "emptied the cities and marched Cambodians to the countryside to starve," and troubles and genocide began only with the KR takeover (ed., April 17, 1998).

Many editorialists and commentators did refer to Pol Pot's Maoist and Parisian ideological training as influencing his behavior, but not his and the Khmer Rouge's experience under the first phase bombings. An exceptionally sleazy editorial in the *Boston Globe* (April 17, 1998) states that Pol Pot, "having half-absorbed the history of the French Revolution and the tenets of the French left while a student in Paris, returned to his native land determined to outdo Maoism in the name of equality," but the editorial never mentions any on-the-ground events before April 1975 that might have affected Khmer Rouge behavior. Stephen Morris, in an Op Ed in the *New York Times* (April 17, 1998), refers to the bombings, but only to deny their influence, arguing that as the Vietnamese were also bombed heavily but didn't kill on a large scale, this demonstrates that it was Communist ideology that explains Pol Pot's killings (although why the Vietnamese, also Communists, didn't kill for reasons of their ideology is not explained)....

GOOD OR BAD GENOCIDIST?

The media handled the U.S. "tilt" toward Pol Pot mainly by evasion, essentially blacking out the years 1979-1995, or vaguely intimating that the U.S. had supported him for reasons of "realpolitik," but quickly moving on without giving details as to the nature and magnitude of support or offering any reflections on the morality of backing "another Hitler." The *New York Times'* April 17 summary of "Pol Pot's Rise and Fall" lists for "1979-1990: Pol Pot and Khmer Rouge are given refuge at Thai border where they fight back against the Vietnamese." "Given refuge" is dishonest: they were given substantial economic and military aid and political support....

Pol Pot was described in the editorials and news columns of April 1998 as "crazed," a "killer," "war criminal," "mass murderer," "blood-soaked," and as having engineered a "reign of terror" and "genocide." Suharto has been in the news in 1998 also, as Indonesia is in a financial crisis and has been negotiating with banks and the International Monetary Fund (IMF) for loans. But during this crisis, and in earlier years as well, while Suharto is occasionally referred to as a "dictator" and running an "authoritarian" regime, he is often a "moderate" and even "at heart benign" *(London Economist),* never a "killer" or "mass murderer" or one responsible for "genocide." The linguistic double standard is maintained reliably throughout the mainstream media....

18

A GENOCIDAL REGIME: THE POINT

David P. Chandler

David P. Chandler was a U.S. Foreign Service Officer in Phnom Penh from 1960-62. He has taught Southeast Asian history at Monash University in Melbourne and served as the Research Director at the University's Centre of Southeast Asian Studies.

■ **POINTS TO CONSIDER**

1. Describe the policies and actions of the Khmer Rouge regime after it took power in 1975.

2. Evaluate the sundry interpretations of the Pol Pot years. Which view does Chandler hold?

3. Chandler is critical of the characterization of Pol Pot and his regime as genocidal. Explain. What term does the author use to classify the regime?

4. Identify the forerunners or parallels to the regime in Cambodia, according to Chandler.

Excerpted from David P. Chandler, **Brother Number One: A Political Biography of Pol Pot,** Boulder, CO: Westview Press, 1992. Used by permission of Westview Press.

Much of what has been written about Pol Pot since his time in power has been reckless and intemperate. This is unsurprising in view of the impact of the revolution; but calling him a "moon-faced monster," a "genocidal maniac," or "worse than Hitler" has no explanatory power.

On April 17, 1975, Cambodia emerged from five traumatic years of invasions, bombardment, and civil war when its capital, Phnom Penh, fell to the guerrilla armies known as the Red Khmer, which had been besieging it since the beginning of the year. The city's population included over one million refugees, driven from their homes in rural areas. During the course of the civil war, half a million Cambodians were killed. People in the cities, without knowing much about the Red Khmer, presumed that peace would be better than war and that Cambodians, working together, could reconstruct their country.

SOCIAL TRANSFORMATION

What happened next took everyone but the Red Khmer commanders by surprise. Within a week, the people of Phnom Penh, Battambang, and other cities were driven into the countryside by the Red Khmer and told to take up agricultural tasks. Thousands of evacuees, especially the very young and the very old, died over the next few weeks. Some survivors, walking toward regions where they hoped their relatives would welcome them, were on the road for over a month. When they asked questions of the heavily armed young soldiers who accompanied them, they were told to obey the "revolutionary organization" *(angkar padevat),* which would act as their "mother and father." The evacuees were called "new people" or "April 17 people" because they had joined the revolution so late. Residents of the countryside were known as "base people" and were treated less harshly than the others.

After emptying the cities, the revolutionary organization embarked on a program of social transformation that affected every aspect of Cambodian life. Money, markets, and private property were abolished. Schools, universities, and Buddhist monasteries were closed. No publishing was allowed; the postal system was abolished; freedom of movement, exchanging information, personal adornment, and leisure activities were curtailed.

Punishments for infractions were severe, and repeat offenders were imprisoned under harsh conditions or killed. Everyone was asked to perform tasks set for them by the revolutionary organization. For evacuee city dwellers, these tasks seldom had any relation to their training or skills. Instead, nearly all of them became peasants and were made to wear identical black cotton clothing.

THE ORGANIZATION

The movement's leaders and their rationale remained concealed. To the outside world Cambodia was still ostensibly ruled by the United Front government, founded in Beijing in 1970 when Prince Norodom Sihanouk, Cambodia's Chief of State, had been overthrown in a bloodless coup while he was abroad, replaced by a government that sought an alliance with the United States. The prince had been the figurehead leader of the resistance in Beijing. By 1972 the Red Khmer controlled the resistance but for the sake of international respectability continued to operate behind the facade of Sihanouk's coalition.

The charade continued for the remainder of 1975. In January 1976 the revolutionary organization dissolved the United Front, changed the name of the country to Democratic Kampuchea (DK), and promulgated a new constitution. The document praised collective values, identified the revolutionary organization with the people's interests, and formalized the collectivization of Cambodian life. The words *socialism* or *communism* appeared nowhere in the text. Soon after, Radio Phnom Penh announced that elections would be held for a national assembly and broadcast the names of ministers in the new regime. The elections, it seemed, were primarily for overseas consumption. "New people" were not allowed to vote; "base people" voted for candidates provided by the organization.

Most of the winners were unknown outside the Red Khmer movement, although some of the new ministers, such as Ieng Sary, Khieu Samphan, and Hu Nim, were prominent leftists who had joined the resistance against Sihanouk in the 1960s. Others elected were identified sooner or later as veteran revolutionaries.

The prime minister, a rubber plantation worker called Pol Pot, was impossible to identify. At the moment he took power, just when he might have been expected to step into the open, he concealed himself behind a revolutionary name....

Mystery clung to him as news of what was happening in Cambodia between 1975 and 1978 — the DK period — filtered into the outside world. Most of the news was horrible. Refugees spoke of forced labor, starvation, random executions, and the tyrannical, anonymous "Organization."...

EXPLAINING THE VIOLENCE

This handful of men and women presided over the purest and most thoroughgoing Marxist-Leninist movement in an era of revolutions. No other regime tried to go so quickly or so far. No other inflicted as many casualties on the country's population.

At one level, the revolution was a courageous, doomed attempt by a group of Utopian thinkers to break free from the capitalist world system, abandon the past, and rearrange the future. Radicals in other countries interpreted events in Cambodia in this way. At another level, the revolution sprang from a colossal misreading of Cambodia's political capacities, its freedom of maneuver *vis-à-vis* its neighbors, and the interests of the rural poor on whose behalf the revolution was ostensibly being waged. At a third level, Pol Pot and his colleagues displayed a thirst for power and an unlimited capacity for distrust. Believing himself surrounded by enemies — a view he shared with, and may have derived from, Stalin — Pol Pot approved the torture and execution of almost twenty thousand enemies *(khmang)* at the regime's interrogation facility in Phnom Penh, known by the code name S-21. And thousands more died in the regional purges he set in motion in 1977. Most of those put to death at S-21 were loyal members of the party. Victims elsewhere, for the most part, seem to have been innocent of treason.

What was the source of the revolution and its extraordinary violence? Between 1975 and 1979, those in power in Phnom Penh frequently declared that they followed no foreign models and that the Cambodian revolution was incomparable. In fact, many DK slogans — such as "storming attacks," "leaps forward," "independence-mastery," and "three tons (of rice) per hectare" — came without acknowledgment from Communist China, where the regime, on the eve of Mao Zedong's death, was going through a peculiarly radical phase.

What the Cambodian leaders meant by independence, in large part, was that they were different from, and superior to, Vietnam, whose Communist movement had shaped and guided them throughout the 1950s and 1960s. Vietnamese guidance began to grate on Saloth Sar and his colleagues in the 1960s, when the Vietnamese treated them not as revolutionaries but as younger brothers in their all-absorbing war against the United States. Fighting between Cambodia and Vietnam erupted in 1977 and culminated two years later in a Vietnamese *blitzkrieg,* which overthrew Pol Pot's regime.

AUTOGENOCIDE

The mayhem that Democratic Kampuchea inflicted on its people led the French author Jean Lacouture to coin the word *autogenocide* — to differentiate events in Cambodia from previous pogroms, holocausts, purges, and vendettas. Lacouture's horror, if not the word he coined, was justified by the facts. In less than four years, more than one million Cambodians, or one in seven, probably died from malnutrition, overwork, and misdiagnosed or mistreated illness. At least 100,000, and probably more, were executed for crimes against the state. Tens of thousands perished in the conflict with Vietnam, almost certainly started by the Red Khmer. But was what happened autogenocide, without forerunners elsewhere? Clear parallels, and probably inspirations, can be found in China's Great Leap Forward in the 1950s, the Soviet collectivization of Ukraine twenty years before that, and purges in both countries of "elements" considered dangerous to revolutionary leaders. In a sense, what happened in Cambodia, although more intense, was standard operating procedure in countries whose politics Pol Pot — or "Brother Number One," as he was informally known to subordinates — admired....

Much of what has been written about Pol Pot since his time in power has been reckless and intemperate. This is unsurprising in view of the impact of the revolution; but calling him a "moon-faced monster," a "genocidal maniac," or "worse than Hitler" (phrases picked from journalists' reports) has no explanatory power. To understand the man, and what happened in DK, it is crucial to place him inside his own Cambodian context and inside a wider set of influences from abroad....

READING

19

A GENOCIDAL REGIME: THE COUNTERPOINT

Sidney H. Schanberg

Sidney H. Schanberg won a Pulitzer Prize for his reporting from Cambodia for The New York Times.

■ POINTS TO CONSIDER

1. What is a Kramar? What comparison does Schanberg make using the Kramar?

2. Describe the kind of purity that the Pol Pot regime desired.

3. Does the author believe the regime was genocidal? Explain.

4. Contrast this reading with the previous reading.

Those who contend that what befell the Khmer people under Pol Pot from 1975 to 1979 cannot technically be called genocide because it was Khmers killing other Khmers, not someone trying to destroy a different race or ethnic group, are arguing semantics, not reality.

The Communists who laid waste to Cambodia and its people in the name of an agrarian revolution used the same purification doctrines that all genocidal regimes have employed. The nation, they decreed, had to be cleansed of all who were not *borisot* — pure. This wasn't merely a reference to Cambodia's ethnic minorities (the Chinese, Vietnamese and Islamic Chams); it applied equally to the entire majority population, the Khmers. The story of Cambodia under the Khmer Rouge is as chilling, insane and incredible as that of any genocide in history. By massacre, forced marches, slave labor, starvation and disease, at least 1.5 million Cambodians were killed in the less than four years the Khmer Rouge held power — roughly 20 percent of the country's eight million. Those who contend that what befell the Khmer people under Pol Pot from 1975 to 1979 cannot technically be called genocide because it was Khmers killing other Khmers, not someone trying to destroy a different race or ethnic group, are arguing semantics, not reality....

DEMOCRATIC KAMPUCHEA

As a correspondent for *The New York Times,* I covered the 1970-75 war between the Washington-backed Cambodian government of Lon Nol and the Beijing-backed Khmer Rouge. My Cambodian colleague Dith Pran and I, along with two million Phnom Penh residents, watched the Khmer Rouge march victoriously into the capital on April 17, 1975. For a few hours, it seemed the takeover would be peaceful, that reconciliation between the two warring sides was possible. The people welcomed the black-garbed Khmer Rouge with flowers and shouts of *"C'est la paix."* Then the crackdown came. Everyone was ordered to the countryside. Those who resisted were shot. Khmer Rouge troops even cleaned out the hospitals; desperately wounded patients were forced into the streets, their serum bottles still attached. The lucky ones had relatives to carry them or push them on their beds. Soon the main boulevards leading out of the city were blanketed curb to curb with traumatized Cambodians head-

Illustration by Kitty Kennedy. Reproduced by permission.

ing into the unknown. So densely packed were the throngs that sandals and shoes came off in the jostling. When after three or four days the city finally emptied and fell silent, the abandoned footwear lay on the streets as a surrealistic reminder that people had actually been there....

To keep the population calm, the Khmer Rouge said the swift evacuation was necessary because the enemy was going to bomb the cities and towns if people stayed bunched up in them. All of this was sham. Pol Pot's true reason for evacuating not just Phnom Penh but every population center in the country was to weed out and *komtec* ("smash," meaning kill) any possible opposition — such as senior officers from the defeated Lon Nol army, former members of the Phnom Penh government, the educated and "soft" classes, monks and others in the pivotal Buddhist religious community, and so on. Dissidents might be able to hide in the cities and province towns, but would be exposed and vulnerable in the countryside. And they would be exposed permanently, for the evacuation was permanent....

The name of the new nation was Democratic Kampuchea. It can best be described as a giant prison, a forced-labor camp the size of Wisconsin. The institution of the family, the core of Cambodian life, was shattered: children were taken from their parents and indoctrinated against them. Schools were shut down, money was abolished, factories left to rust, pagodas razed and the monks either killed or set to hard labor in the fields. Anything foreign was regarded as tainted and therefore cause for punishment, even execution — including knowledge of a foreign language. Newspapers and television stations ceased to exist and radio sets were taken away. Except for China and a handful of other Communist nations like Albania and North Korea, no embassies were allowed. And no foreign journalists were let in. In short, the country was sealed. The world could not look in. The killing could begin....

THE CENTER

[T]he "Center" — Pol Pot and his circle of loyalists — dealt with any hint of resistance and imposed its fierce control. One method was mass purges; no one was to be trusted. (A Khmer Rouge slogan went: "Spare them, no profit — Destroy them, no loss.") Another was the deportation of whole sections of the population, frequently thousands at a time, to districts far away. Sometimes deportees would be given specially colored pieces of clothing, blue-and-white-checked *Kramar,* a traditional rough-cotton neckerchief and sweatband used for everything from carrying produce to serving as a cover garment for bathing in the river The deportees soon realized that the *Kramar* was not a gift but a neon sign, identifying them as disloyal Khmers to be singled out for harsh treatment or elimination. The blue scarves were Pol Pot's Stars of David.

Many deportees were people shipped out of the Eastern Zone, where the local Khmer Rouge leadership had come under suspicion for what the Center regarded as "soft" views and a reluctance at times to carry out the Center's harshest edicts. The Eastern Zone's proximity to Vietnam also made its people suspect, for despite support for the Khmer Rouge in the early years, Hanoi had come to be viewed by the Center as a stone-cold enemy, and Pol Pot had instigated a border war to try to seize Vietnamese territory that had been part of the Khmer empire centuries ago. Exiles to northwestern provinces wearing the blue scarves were called "Khmer bodies with Vietnamese minds."...

DARK MEMORIES

Of course, the massacres were hardly confined to people of the Eastern Zone. Every corner of Cambodia had its killing fields. And

DESTRUCTION OF TIBET

Since the 24-year-old Dalai Lama went into exile 40 years ago, more than 80,000 Tibetans have joined the refugee communities he founded in India, Nepal, and Bhutan.

They have fled from genocide. By its own estimate, between March of 1959 and October of 1960, the People's Liberation Army killed over 87,000 Tibetans in Central Tibet alone....

The current estimate is that more than 1.2 million Tibetans are dead as a result of the Chinese occupation....

Tendzin Choegyal, "The Truth about Tibet," **Imprimus,** April 1999.

indeed, as resistance born of desperation finally began to stir in the countryside, Pol Pot was soon seeing spies and traitors everywhere. He started purging sections of his own army, and then even members of his ruling group. A growing number of Khmer Rouge soldiers headed into the bush to become guerrillas against the Center. Some units defected to Vietnam. It was 1978, and Pol Pot's bloody dominion was unraveling....

To this day, years after the Vietnamese invaded and drove the Khmer Rouge into the jungle, thousands of Cambodians are still the psychiatric walking wounded. It is not an uncommon sight to see someone riding a bicycle down a busy Phnom Penh street suddenly lose control, veer off and smack into a parked car. Without warning a dark memory from those inhuman years has slipped unwanted into the cyclist's mind and stunned his senses. There is no cure. Time only softens some effects....

RECOGNIZING AUTHOR'S POINT OF VIEW

This activity may be used as an individualized study guide for students in libraries and resource centers or as a discussion catalyst in small group and classroom discussions.

The capacity to recognize an author's point of view is an essential reading skill. Many readers do not make clear distinctions between descriptive articles that relate factual information and articles that express a point of view. Think about the readings in chapter three. Choose one of the following source descriptions that best defines each source in chapter three.

Source Descriptions

a. Essentially an article that relates factual information

b. Essentially an article that expresses editorial points of view

c. Both of the above

d. Neither of the above

Readings in Chapter Three

_____ Reading Fourteen
"Inside Pol Pot's Cambodia, 1975-1979" by John Barron

_____ Reading Fifteen
"Killing Birds: The U.S. and Cambodia, 1969-1973"
by Ben Kiernan

_____ Reading Sixteen
"Pot Pot's Death and His Place in History"
by Jeffrey Hart

_____ Reading Seventeen
"Pol Pot's Death and His Place in Media"
by Edward S. Herman

_____ Reading Eighteen
"A Genocidal Regime: The Point" by David P. Chandler

_____ Reading Nineteen
"A Genocidal Regime: The Counterpoint"
by Sidney Schanberg

2. Summarize the author's point of view in one to three sentences for each of the readings in Chapter Three.

3. After careful consideration, pick out one reading that you think is the most reliable source. Be prepared to explain the reasons for your choice in a general class discussion.

CHAPTER 4

NEVER AGAIN? COMMITMENT TO STOP RWANDAN GENOCIDE

READING

20

THE CAUSES OF RWANDAN GENOCIDE: ETHNIC RIVALRY

Yenwith K. Whitney

Yenwith K. Whitney is the former Associate for Africa of the Presbyterian Church (USA). He is now retired.

■ **POINTS TO CONSIDER**

1. What happened in Rwanda in April 1994?

2. Explain the nature of the "conflict," according to the author.

3. Discuss the difficulties facing post-genocide Rwanda.

4. Evaluate the statement, "These people [Hutus] were brought up…to believe that it was okay to kill Tutsis." Compare this reading with Daniel Goldhagen's (Reading Three).

Excerpted from Yenwith K. Whitney, "Rwanda: The Tragedy Continues," **World Updates,** vol. 8, no. 4, Fall 1998. Reprinted with permission from Presbyterian Church (USA) United Nations Office.

This historic ethnic rivalry goes back hundreds of years.

The events of April 1994 are some of the most tragic that have ever occurred on the African continent. How nearly a million people could be slaughtered in 100 days without any intervention on the part of the outside world is a question that should trouble the consciences of all nations, not least our own. By and large the outside world remained ignorant of the horrifying details and magnitude of the slaughter, a slaughter equal to that which occurred in Indonesia in the 1960s....

Flying in to Rwanda one is impressed by the peaceful rolling hills and pastoral scenes that come into view as you approach Kigali, Rwanda's capital. But this serenity belies the turmoil that pervades a troubled land.

ETHNIC RIVALRY

Rwanda's troubles did not start on April 6, 1994, when a missile fired from the swamps outside of the perimeter of the Kigali airport downed a transport plane, killing President Juvenal Habyarimana. This historic ethnic rivalry goes back hundreds of years to a time when the pastoral Tutsis, migrating south into the volcanic highlands of central Africa, subjugated the agricultural Hutus. In the latter part of the nineteenth century, the Belgian colonial government gave administrative responsibilities over the country to the Tutsis. This further reinforced what the Hutus perceived as the Tutsi sense of superiority. The Tutsis continued the traditional domination by reserving the best in educational and job opportunities for their own ethnic group. The Tutsis and the Hutus lived in constant and precarious tension.

In 1959, on the eve of independence from colonial rule, the Hutus ousted the Tutsi leadership. The newly independent government sanctioned an ideology that considered the Tutsi "foreign invaders" who should be sent back to Ethiopia.

The consensus now is that Hutu radicals had prepared elaborate plans for the genocide months ahead of the downing of the President's airplane. A short time prior to the incident, President Habyarimana, a moderate Hutu, negotiated a power sharing agreement with the Tutsi rebels which had infuriated the Hutu radicals. After the airplane crash, the Hutus orchestrated a

144

Cartoon by Richard Wright.

well-planned campaign to massacre the Tutsis whom they blamed for the death of Mr. Habyarimana. In the succeeding 100 days, the Hutu-led genocide claimed an estimated 800,000 victims while the outside world looked on, taking no action.

When the Tutsi army, which had reorganized in Uganda under the sympathetic eye of President Museveni, drove out the Hutu government, the world breathed a collective sigh of relief. The Hutus fled to Zaire. It appeared that the brutal slaughter was finished. The world was only too happy to send in supplies and aid workers to help the beleaguered government reestablish itself.

Although the darkest days of genocide have passed, killing continues....

THREE HUNDRED YEARS UNTIL JUSTICE?

The task of the current government, a coalition of Tutsis and Hutus, seems almost impossible. Rwanda faces the monumental task of defusing murderous ethnic hatred in a country where these people still live side-by-side as neighbors. There are no enclaves as there are in the former Yugoslavia or Ireland where ethnic groups can live separated from their antagonists. Rwanda's government must try to bring peace between the Tutsis and Hutus and at the same time bring a sense of justice to the survivors who have suffered such great losses.

Thousands have been arrested in Rwanda, implicated in the massacres. Rwandan prisons are holding more than 130,000 prisoners waiting for trials. The system is so overwhelmed that one estimate is that it would take 300 years to resolve all the cases. The prisoners, who are mostly Hutus, do not believe that they will ever get justice from this government which is dominated by Tutsis.

A 1996 law permits confessions and plea-bargaining, the latter a novel concept in Rwanda. Those who confess get speedier trials and if convicted of the severest crimes are promised life sentences rather than execution. Prisoners take this law seriously since the execution of 22 people in April 1998. This year more than 8,000 have confessed — mainly lesser ranking people rather than those political and military leaders who organized the massacres.

One of the great challenges facing Rwanda and its people is a lack of contrition — the understanding that what happened there was so monumentally evil that it cannot be rationalized in a civilized world. A justice official observed: "They are prepared to say they're sorry but there's no remorse at all. This is not surprising. These people were brought up for 30 years to believe that it was okay to kill Tutsis." The genocide was a justifiable act to defeat a non-native enemy — to drive the Tutsi "cockroaches" from Rwanda....

READING

21

THE CAUSES OF RWANDAN GENOCIDE: POLITICAL POWER

Alan Zarembo

Alan Zarembo writes frequently on Africa. During his studies in Africa, he wrote a thesis on the Ugandan-sponsored Rwandan Patriotic Front invasion of 1990. Zarembo visited a Rwandan prison in October 1994, three months after Tutsi rebels took power in Rwanda to end the genocide.

■ POINTS TO CONSIDER

1. Describe the author's view of the ethnic differences between Hutus and Tutsis in Rwanda.

2. Explain the role the Belgians played in Rwandan history. What is the legacy of the Belgians, according to Zarembo?

3. Discuss the author's opinion of the cause of the genocide.

4. Evaluate the impact of obedience in driving the genocide. Is this an appropriate explanation or an excuse?

The genocide had less to do with whether ordinary Hutus believed killing their Tutsi neighbors was a good idea than with upholding the standards of good citizenship, which in the spring and early summer of 1994 was to kill Tutsis in broad daylight.

...Anyone who saw mutilated bodies flicker across a television screen in the spring of 1994 might dismiss the genocide as yet another African tribal war unleashed in yet another lawless African state. Hutus make up 85 percent of the population; Tutsis, most of the rest. But the problem is that there is little consensus about whether Hutus and Tutsis can be called tribes at all. Before colonialism, Rwanda was a highly organized feudal kingdom. The overlords were Tutsis, but not all Tutsis were privileged. The two groups meet none of the standard conditions that define tribes; for centuries they have lived on the same hillsides, spoken the same language, shared the same burial customs, and intermarried.

ETHNOLOGY

The Belgians, masters of Rwanda and neighboring Burundi for four decades, tried to quantify the differences between Hutus and Tutsis. Belgian ethnologists claimed that the average Tutsi nose was 55.8 millimeters long and 38.7 millimeters wide, compared with Hutu dimensions of 52.4 and 43.2. Other dubious distinctions were based on property: those who owned fewer than ten cows were said to be Hutus; the rest, Tutsis. The colonial government issued each group identity cards and forced Hutus to work for free while Tutsis supervised. The first massacres in Rwanda erupted in 1959, when Hutus slaughtered Tutsis in order to consolidate power before the country's pending independence in 1962. Roving the hillsides in squads, they chased tens of thousands of Tutsis into exile, the same Tutsis who would multiply in asylum, creating a generation of expatriates who would return to take power after the 1994 genocide.

ORDER

Far from being another lawless African country, independent Rwanda became and remains a model of order. The country is divided in 12 prefectures, 154 communes, 1,600 sectors, and tens of thousands of cellules — a top-down network of officialdom rooted in a precolonial kingdom, codified by colonizers, and preserved after independence. Once Hutus had vanquished the Tutsi elite, it used the pre-existing social structure to exercise complete control over the populace. Residents had to ask permission to leave their hillsides. Everybody became a *de facto* member of the only political party, Hutu President-for-Life Juvenal Habyarimana's *Mouvement Revolutionnaire National pour le Dévelopment* (MRND). When opposition parties were legalized in 1991, MRND tacked *"et la Démocratie"* to its name, but nothing about Rwanda was very democratic. It was a nation of followers, a culture that foreign-aid donors believed contributed to progress: more than 60 percent of Rwandans were Catholics, a higher proportion than anywhere else on the continent; there was very little street crime; and peasants spent two days a month planting trees, terracing fields, and paving roads in a national service program called *umuganda,* which amounted to forced labor. The crews were called *Interhamwe:* those who work together.

Foreigners refused to see the bigger national project in the pipeline. They could have looked for clues in Burundi, where over the last three decades the Tutsi minority had kept their grip on power by periodically massacring Hutus, as many as 300,000 in 1972. Both countries have the same ethnic mix, but lacking the revolution that brought Hutus to power in Rwanda, Hutus in Burundi had grown so obedient to their Tutsi overlords that they dug their own graves and reported to police stations for their scheduled — and sometimes rescheduled — executions. Some twenty-two years later in Rwanda, it was Tutsis who would die, and this time it would be the civic duty of Hutus to kill them. The ideology of Tutsi extermination would flow down the hierarchy of command into virtually every home, the churches would fill with bodies, the terraced fields would become mass graves, Hutu soldiers would speed across the country on some of the best roads in Africa, pink identity cards would help determine who would live and who would die, and *Interhamwe* would refer to a new kind of work crew: not tree planters but militias made up of peasants and unemployed young men recruited from the ranks of ordinary Hutus on every hillside, the gangs that became the most notoriously brutal killers.

SEEDS OF GENOCIDE

The seeds of genocide were planted in late 1990, shortly after the Rwandan Patriotic Front (RPF), a rebel army led by English-speaking Tutsi refugees, invaded from Uganda. Three years of fighting ended in a stalemate, forcing the MRND to sign a power-sharing agreement with the Tutsi RPF rebels. But the Hutu leaders delayed implementing the agreement, and extremists within the government began to enact a plan to exterminate not only all Tutsis but Hutu sympathizers as well.[1] On April 6, 1994, President Habyarimana's plane was shot down — most likely by his own extremist Hutu allies — killing him and providing the pretext for the massacres.

Enlisting civilians to kill was a deliberate attempt by the ruling Hutus to create a society that Tutsis could never govern. And it may have worked. Although in 1994 the RPF defeated the Hutu army, stopped the genocide, and took power,[2] the only beneficiaries of their revolution so far have been the army officers who claimed hillside villas and the roughly 800,000 Tutsi refugees who returned from three decades in exile to replace the dead. The RPF set up a coalition government that blames tribal distinctions on colonialism and avoids using the words "Hutu" and "Tutsi," but few believe the pretense of kinship. Hutus in the government are figureheads; intermarriage has all but ceased; and Hutu extremists still kill Tutsi survivors and foreigners as part of ongoing attempts to destabilize the Tutsi-led government. Many of the estimated six million Hutus view their new bosses as a foreign army of occupation. Imagine the Jews picking up arms in 1945, taking over Germany, and then having to run the country.

But even this comparison falls short. At the height of the Holocaust in 1944, the Nazis executed about 400,000 over a three-month period, the same length of time it took Hutus to kill twice that many. If Nazis ran killing factories that most Germans never had to confront directly, Rwandans murdered intimately, spattering their clothes with the blood of their neighbors....

OBEDIENCE AND HEALING

You too might obey orders to kill even if you believed killing was morally wrong — for example, to save your own life. That is not what happened in Rwanda. The genocide happened so swiftly, with so little internal resistance, that there was no time for a national moral dilemma. Some killers proved themselves equally capable of good and evil, hiding Tutsis by night, butchering them by day. The genocide had less to do with whether ordinary Hutus believed killing their Tutsi neighbors was a good idea than with upholding the standards of good citizenship, which in the spring

ARMS FOR RWANDA

Although exact numbers are unknown, Kalashnikov rifles have been flooding markets and wars throughout Africa and Asia. As late as March 1992 belligerents in Central Africa could pick them up in bulk for $220 each; prices have since dropped well below $200. In countries like Rwanda, Kalashnikovs were once more common than cars; now they are more common than bicycles. About 80 percent of the weapons used by the RPF guerrillas were Kalashnikovs, many of Romanian manufacture....

Frank Smyth, "Blood Money and Geopolitics," **The Nation,** 2 May 1994.

and early summer of 1994 was to kill Tutsis in broad daylight. Ironically, such civic devotion may be the only chance for healing Rwanda. The idea is less absurd, and more hopeful, than is the fatalistic myth of Rwandans as a people forever condemned to follow feral impulses....

It is the reason why few genocide survivors have sought revenge, why pedestrians stand at attention and rush-hour traffic stops when the Rwandan flag is raised and lowered, why the once bloodied churches fill up again every Sunday, why Rwandans still come by the thousands when the government radio announces *umuganda* workdays, why genocide suspects are allowed to use machetes, why some prison fences are made of eucalyptus branches, and why inmates applaud for the government ministers who imprisoned them.

The "law" that the returned prisoners are talking about is not a permanent set of ethics written in the Rwandan criminal code or the Bible but the directives of whoever is currently in power. And in that sense, Rwandans are among the most law-abiding citizens in the world. The genocide was not an eruption of tribalism but the rote conduct of a society raised on reverence for even the most wicked leaders. Killing was the law, and Rwandans followed it.

NOTES FOR READING TWENTY-ONE

1 Extremists pushed an ideology known as Hutu Power *via* propaganda such as *Kangura,* a magazine that in 1990 published "The Hutu 10 Commandments," which warned Hutus not to intermarry, fraternize, or go into business with Tutsis. Commandment 8 states simply, "The Hutu should stop having mercy on the Tutsi." Commandment 10 proclaims that "the Hutu Ideology must be taught to every Hutu at every level...Any Hutu who persecutes his brother Hutu for having read, spread, and taught this ideology is a traitor."

2 Ironically, the downfall of the Hutu regime may have been due to its dedication of men and resources to the genocide rather than to fighting the highly disciplined RPF, which forced the Hutu army and militias into exile in Zaire.

READING

22

THE CAUSES OF RWANDAN GENOCIDE: ECONOMICS

Emmanuel Ohajah

Emmanuel Ohajah is a Nigerian writer based in London.

■ **POINTS TO CONSIDER**

1. Explain Ohajah's view of the root source of the violence in Rwanda and other parts of Africa.

2. How are African societies portrayed, particularly in Western media? Are these fair characterizations?

3. Analyze the contention that African nations are incapable of self-governance.

Excerpted from Emmanuel Ohajah, "Economics, Not Tribalism Is Cause of Bloodbath in Rwanda," as it appeared in the **Star Tribune,** 15 April 1994, Reprinted with permission, Pacific News Service.

The real problems are economic and social ones, not tribalism.

The entire world is told by the media — mostly Western or Western-controlled — that tribal factions have turned Rwanda into a bloodbath, with rival mobs hacking their victims to death. It would seem that all of Rwanda's problems can be put down to a bloodlust peculiar to Africans.

SCARCE RESOURCES

Yet for Africans and those who know the region there is only one root source of the violence: More and more people are competing for fewer and fewer resources. The struggle for ever scarcer resources — and as a direct consequence for political power — is what fuels conflicts in Rwanda, Burundi and elsewhere in Africa. The real problems are economic and social ones, not tribalism.

Each year sub-Saharan Africa repays its Western creditors ten billion dollars (US), more than four times the amount the region spends on health and education. The International Monetary Fund (IMF) has not helped the situation: It has regularly taken two billion dollars more in interest payments than it has provided in loans since 1987. This flow of wealth, from south to north, has resulted in a decline in new investment in industry and the basic infrastructure of society.

The collapse in the prices of key African exports such as tea, coffee and tin has combined with the wealth outflow to create major hardship throughout central Africa. Coffee prices have fallen by more than 34 percent over the past decade. Rwanda is vitally dependent on this commodity, and neighboring Burundi receives more than 80 percent of its revenue from coffee.

But the endless drumbeat in the Western media about the moral crisis in African society seems more than sensationalist pandering to TV viewers and newspaper readers. From South Africa to Algeria, African societies are presented as depraved and degenerate. Images of Somali warlords who steal food from aid agencies merge into those of black township youths with necklaces of burning tires and Islamic fundamentalists in the Sudan who crucify Christians at every opportunity.

IMF AND WORLD BANK

In November 1990, barely six weeks after the rebel army of the Rwandan Patriotic Front (RPF) launched its civil war, the government, acting on IMF policy recommendations, imposed a 50 percent devaluation of the Rwandan franc, along with sizeable increases in the prices of fuel and consumer essentials. Touted as a way to increase coffee exports and rehabilitate the war-ravaged economy, the measures had exactly the opposite effect. From a situation of relative stability, inflation soared, real earnings declined, state enterprises went into bankruptcy, child malnutrition rose, and health and education collapsed under the austerity measures....

In June 1992, at the height of the civil war, the IMF ordered a second devaluation....

Michel Chossudovsky, "IMF and World Bank Set the Stage," **Covert Action Quarterly,** Spring 1995.

PROPAGANDA ONSLAUGHT

The unspoken conclusion all this reporting leads to is that Africa is intent on tearing itself apart and therefore is incapable of governing itself.

This is not the first time Africa has been the target of this kind of propaganda onslaught. During the 1950s and '60s African liberation movements were the targets of incessant vilification. When the movements sought to break out of this stranglehold, the media of the colonial powers struck back by calling into question their ability to govern themselves.

Today, with the end of the Cold War, the West is grappling with the loss of its own moral certainties even as its moral authority is being challenged throughout the non-Western world. In this context intervention in Africa, whether rhetorical, political or military, offers Westerners an opportunity to walk tall again.

The sovereignty of African states is being questioned more and more. Calls to suspend sovereignty, couched in the language of humanitarianism, have already been voiced in regard to Somalia and now Rwanda. If Africans are not careful, colonialism will be back in Africa before you can say "white man's burden."

READING

23

INTERVENTION: THE CHURCH'S RESPONSE

Carole Collins

Former National Catholic Reporter *Diplomatic Correspondent Carole J.L. Collins is currently National Coordinator of Jubilee 2000 USA. She has written on African issues for more than 20 years, and is a former Southern Africa International Affairs Representative of the American Friends Service Committee.*

■ POINTS TO CONSIDER

1. Identify the cause of the violence, according to the article.

2. What did the church do to stop the genocide?

3. Discuss how the church abetted the tragedy, according to the author.

Excerpted from Carole Collins, "Church Abetted Tragedy in Rwanda, Priest Says," **National Catholic Reporter,** 7 October 1994. Reprinted with permission of Carole Collins.

The church also failed to "engage itself in effective struggle for justice and reconciliation.

Why did the Catholic church do so little to stop the genocidal carnage in Rwanda? How could such violence occur in a country where 90 percent of the people are Christian and 62 percent call themselves Catholic, where the Catholic church was, "after the government, the single most powerful institution"?

These are the uncomfortable but compelling questions posed by the Association of Member Episcopal Conferences in Eastern Africa. AMECEA groups the Catholic bishops' conferences from eight poverty-stricken nations in this conflict-riven region: Eritrea, Ethiopia, Kenya, Malawi, Sudan, Uganda, Tanzania and Zambia.

ETHNIC TENSIONS AMONG CLERGY

Father Wolfgang Schonecke [is] a member of the German Missionaries of Africa, White Fathers, who worked with Rwandans for many years in Uganda. In June [1994] he was designated the secretary — and first head — of AMECEA's pastoral department, set up to assist AMECEA members' national pastoral programs and to share pastoral initiatives with those inside and outside the East African region.

The issues raised apply far beyond the borders of the impoverished, Vermont-sized nation in East Africa now infamous for the low-tech slaughter of more than one million civilians contrived by Hutu militias bent on exterminating both Hutu and Tutsi opponents.

Schonecke recounts how ethnic hatred and fear, rooted in a history of reciprocal tensions and periodic pogroms — and exacerbated by Belgian colonial favoritism toward Tutsis — obviously contributed to Rwanda's recent horrors. But he goes on to detail the church's failure to address its own cultural and ethnic tensions, especially among the clergy. "How can we create a true sense of church as family," he asks, "where ethnic, cultural and religious differences are lived as complementarity, not as competition? How can we foster a people's search for cultural identity in society and the church without losing the sense of national unity, of international community and of religious catholicity?"

Contrary to the popular view that the Rwandan tragedy was solely ethnic in origin, Schonecke links the massacres to other

Illustration by Eleanor Mill. Reprinted with permission.

factors, which also call into question the role played by the Catholic church in the Rwandan conflict.

The first of the causes he lists is "an obsession with obtaining and retaining power at any price, including the use of violence." Schonecke chronicles both the former ruling Hutu clique's adamant refusal to share any power with its critics, as well as past anti-civilian violence by the current Tutsi-dominated Rwandan Patriotic Front government, which ousted the former rulers.

COZY RELATIONS

He also details how Rwanda's Catholic hierarchy maintained "cozy relations" with a series of rulers — first the Belgian colonial administration, then the Tutsi royal house and later the Hutu-dominated regime headed by the late President Juvenal Habyarimana — all of whom felt justified in violently repressing their opponents. Indeed, the late Archbishop Vincent Nsengiyumva belonged for years to the Hutu ruling party's central committee which planned the recent genocidal campaigns.

While some church groups worked for justice, human rights and democracy, their efforts were undercut by a hierarchy "too closely linked with the ruling regime to be a credible voice of protest."

"How can the church resist the temptation to use power in its mission and in turn to be used by the political powers?" Schonecke asks. Can it stand apart from the "power struggle of persons and groups and focus on the real and important issues of justice for all?" More pointedly, he asks, "Do we speak up for any group treated unfairly or only when church interests are threatened?"...Can we develop in the church a more participatory style of leadership as a model for a more democratic style of leadership in politics?

SOCIAL PROBLEMS

Schonecke also blames a sense of hopelessness generated by rampant unemployment and the negative social effects of International Monetary Fund programs. The church was once the prime agent of development in Rwanda, Schonecke notes, but it failed to recognize that strong social services don't necessarily ensure either long-term economic development or the building up of true faith communities.

The church also failed to "engage itself in effective struggle for justice and reconciliation, the only long-term basis for true development." Many Rwandan church leaders developed opulent lifestyles, which alienated them from ordinary Christians and made them appear part of Rwanda's exploitative upper classes. Do church institutions "still serve the poor as they were originally meant to?" Schonecke asks. "Are we equally committed to ensure the foundations of justice in society as we are to development projects?"

A growing population fueled the conflict as Rwandans competed for scarce land and other resources, Schonecke says. Past government efforts to encourage family planning were actively opposed by the church on moral grounds in the most densely populated country on earth. Pope John Paul II did not even mention the subject during his visit to Rwanda in 1990, says Schonecke. Yet, "planned parenthood [is] a necessity for families and for the larger community" in many countries. How far is natural family planning, the church's "answer" to this problem, "in fact available to the average Christian couple in our countries?" he asks. "What solutions do we have to offer to couples for whom this method is impossible?"

The horrors were possible, in part, he says, because of deliberate disinformation spread by mass media for conditioning people to accept and commit violence. Radio broadcasts were extensively used by the ruling Hutu clique for "vicious incitement to ethnic violence" and quickly "created a climate of mass hysteria." He writes that pastoral letters, couched in too much theological language, "do not reach the minds of most Christians," and he calls for greater church investment of talent in the media and greater freedom to express cultural values through the media....

THE MODEL OF CHURCH

Rwandan Christians' failure to protect their church leaders or prevent the desecration of their churches and destruction of social institutions calls into question "the model of church Africa has inherited from the missionaries and continues to follow," Schonecke argues. Catholic teaching exalting obedience and reinforcing a traditional culture's emphasis on absolute obedience to authority "maybe made the perversion of power possible."...

INTERVENTION: THE FAILURE OF THE INTERNATIONAL COMMUNITY

Stephen J. Pope

Stephen J. Pope is an Associate Professor of Theology at Boston College.

■ POINTS TO CONSIDER

1. Summarize the response of the international community to the genocide in Rwanda, according to Pope.

2. Analyze the author's response to President Clinton's latest diplomatic gestures in Rwanda.

3. What did powerful nations see as the source of the catastrophe?

4. Do you think racism or Rwanda's poverty caused powerful nations not to react during the genocide?

5. Identify further obstacles the West, particularly the U.S., continues to erect during Rwanda's healing process.

Excerpted from Stephen J. Pope, "The Politics of Apology and Slaughter in Rwanda," **America,** 6 March 1999. Reprinted with permission, **America Press,** Inc.

The United Nations leadership and the entire international community, especially Belgium, France and United States, failed completely in their responsibility during this catastrophe.

...In Rwanda, over the course of 100 days from April to June 1994, Hutu leaders organized a systematic genocide that exterminated about 800,000 Tutsi and moderate Hutu. The slaughter occurred in a country of only seven million people — a killing spree accomplished mostly by machete and clubs that experts have described as five times more "efficient" than that of the Nazis. To be sure, the agents of the murder were the Hutu and especially their leaders. But the United Nations leadership and the entire international community, especially Belgium, France and United States, failed completely in their responsibility during this catastrophe.

DAMNABLE MORAL CHOICES

On March 25, 1998, President Clinton flew to Rwanda to "pay the respects" of our country to the victims of the genocide. He apologized for the failure of the international community to stop the genocide, but he did not take personal moral responsibility for wrongdoing....

The President confessed to what had already been exposed: that the United Nation's leadership, along with the powerful governments of the world, despite all their bold post-Holocaust proclamations of "never again," were bystanders at yet another genocide. He attempted to minimize the accountability of the U.S. Government by word manipulation, shifted blame by feigning ignorance and then later acted in ways that directly contradicted his public proclamations.

The President claimed that "we did not act quickly enough." This can be regarded as literally true, but it falsely suggests that our Government eventually engaged in some significant action. Our policy makers chose, no doubt with a mind to the 18 U.S. Army rangers previously killed in Mogadishu, to resist humanitarian intervention, including the maintenance of secure areas to protect civilians literally begging for their lives. Employing a Reaganesque "mistakes were made" approach, the President did not mention that he himself was responsible for the Administration's decision to work for the removal of the remain-

162

Cartoon by Joel Pett. Reprinted with permission.

ing 1,700 in-country United Nations troops from Rwanda in April [1994] and to oppose Boutros-Ghali's plan to employ a 5,500-strong military force in May. These were damnable moral choices.

PLEADING IGNORANCE

Clinton told the survivors, "We didn't realize the extent or the depth of the evil that was engulfing you." This verbal maneuver tries to evade accountability on the grounds of "invincible ignorance," the claim that one could not have known any better and so is not responsible. Clinton lamented "people like me sitting in offices, day after day after day, who did not fully appreciate the depth and the speed with which you were being engulfed." The suggestion is that Clinton, like most everyone else, did not know, and cannot have been expected to have known, what was going on in far away Rwanda. His apology in effect tried to twist the words into an absolving excuse.

This profession of ignorance did not, of course, advert to later publicized UN cables (especially from General Romeo Dallaire, UN force commander in Rwanda), press reports, International Red Cross bulletins and reports from other nongovernmental organizations, memos from Africa specialists, requests from in-country UN forces and an internal State Department report in April that the killings amounted to genocide. Cables from Kigali in January warned in no uncertain terms that detailed plans had been drawn up for the premeditated genocide of all Tutsi and their allies, and that the Hutu had the means and were looking for the right opportunity to carry out these plans.

This and other available information suggest two scenarios regarding the nature of this "ignorance." One is held by James Woods, deputy assistant secretary for African Affairs at the Department of Defense in 1994, who believes that the information was available but that high ranking U.S. policy makers decided not to pay attention to it: "They chose not to know, and they chose not to act." A second is that they did know but feigned ignorance. The first scenario exemplifies what St. Thomas Aquinas would call "affected ignorance" resulting from moral negligence; the second is a simple case of lying in order to evade accountability for a massive failure of political will. Either alternative is reprehensible.

In the midst of his Rwandan apology the President vowed to provide means for arresting, prosecuting and punishing the murderers. He promised to "increase our vigilance and strengthen our stand against those who would commit such atrocities in the future" and to "maximize the chances of preventing [such] events." In particular, the President specifically committed himself to work for the creation of an international tribunal so that future perpetrators of genocide would have to answer for their acts.

SUPERFICIAL SENTIMENT

Yet four months later, on July 17 [1998], the U.S. delegation in Rome voted against the International Criminal Tribunal that was being created to deal precisely with such crimes against humanity. This delegation implemented the will of the President, who decided not to spend his political capital fighting Senator Jesse Helms (Republican of North Carolina) and his allies in the Senate. To be fair, the U.S. Government has donated significant funds for a human rights tribunal, the training of judicial and police officials and relief efforts in Rwanda. Yet this money does not compensate for the President's active opposition to institutions needed to hold perpetrators of genocide accountable for their crimes.

The refusal to vote in favor of the International Criminal Tribunal places in bold relief the real reason why our Government refused to take this tragedy seriously: Rwanda was not perceived to be of vital concern to our national self-interest. It also underscores in the most graphic way the kind of cheap forgiveness sought by our apologetic President. It is the "most graphic way" because its representative images are not a cigar and a stained dress but countless piles of human corpses strewn along roadsides from one end of this country to another.

This kind of "apology" cannot be dismissed as yet another attempt of the "Comeback Kid" to use superficial sentiment as a means of damage control. It amounted to an alibi for unconscionable negligence and even active obstruction of what any decent person would recognize as a duty to protect people from being massacred. Far from "paying respect," Clinton's speech further insulted its victims and their loved ones.

It is true that we cannot be the "world's policeman," but a realistic sense of our limited power does not make it legitimate for us to turn our backs on the massive numbers of innocent people who were slaughtered. Clinton at least recognizes this, so perhaps his apology can be construed as the tribute vice plays to virtue. Yet if *The New York Times* columnist Maureen Dowd is correct in her judgment that Clinton is "pathologically incorrigible," one of the gravest manifestations of his incorrigibility is the deliberate political manipulation that contributed to the Rwandan catastrophe.

In any case, it is no credit to the American people that we have not been troubled by the deadly consequences surrounding Clinton's falsity and hypocrisy regarding Rwanda. The same principles that in 1994 strangled appeals for humanitarian intervention remain in effect today. Their application points not only to deep flaws in Administration policy and the President's own character but also, and more importantly, to the moral failures of an indifferent society that has not called the President to task.

RESPONSIBILITY AND POWER

This tragedy, at least, should reinforce a lesson already acknowledged by moral common sense: that those with power must take their responsibility to the powerless with grave moral seriousness. We should not allow our consciences to be bought off with a sporadic infusion of aid nor our national guilt to be absolved by inauthentic apologies after the fact. Choreographed prayer breakfasts, photo ops on church steps and orchestrated displays of remorse are no substitute for the courage to tell the truth about one's own wrongdoing. Even less can they substitute for coming to the aid of innocent men, women and children subjected to the abomination of genocide. These commitments will only influence foreign policy when the people of the United States insist that our politicians take them seriously, and will certainly not when we are willing to accept in their place lame and disingenuous apologies from our President.

READING

25

INTERVENTION: GENOCIDE PREVENTION IS NEEDED

Robert J. White

Robert J. White is a staff columnist on foreign affairs for the Star Tribune *of Minneapolis. White wrote his article during the Hutu exodus from Rwanda after the three-month slaughter of Tutsis. Fearing reprisal from the Tutsi-led Rwandan Patriotic Front (RPF), ethnic Hutus fled to Zaire (Democratic Republic of Congo), Tanzania and Burundi. Perhaps one million Hutu refugees were forcibly repatriated in the fall of 1996.*

■ **POINTS TO CONSIDER**

1. What does White identify as the cause of genocide in Rwanda?

2. Describe the dilemma for relief workers after the genocide.

3. Discuss the author's critique of the international community response to the Rwandan genocide.

4. Assess the statement "There is a strong tendency to view all emergencies as if they are the equivalent of natural disaster." What is the author's point in using this quote?

Excerpted from Robert J. White, "Another Genocide Can Be Prevented," **Star Tribune,** 22 December 1994. Reprinted with permission.

Prevention would have cost far less in dollars and lives.

In the summer [1994], the plight of tens of thousands of cholera-stricken Rwandan refugees prompted an outpouring of generosity.

Citizens sent millions of dollars to relief organizations, while the Clinton Administration mounted a massive airlift to deliver shelter, food, medicine and water-purification systems for Rwandan refugees dying in camps in Zaire [Democratic Republic of Congo].

PREVENTING EXODUS

It may seem churlish to point out flaws in this armor of self-congratulation, but ignoring them would be worse.

The largest flaw is this: The United States had the ability, means and influence to prevent the terrible acts that provoked the mass exodus from Rwanda. Prevention would have cost far less in dollars and lives. The Clinton Administration not only declined to lead in prevention, it interfered with efforts of others to do so. Moreover, that conclusion comes not from the wisdom of hindsight; it was evident at the time.

The holiday season would be an inappropriate time to recall the ghosts of tragedies past, were it not for indications that the tragedy will recur. The elements for new massacres are in place. A reminder came recently when the aid organization Doctors Without Borders pulled out of a Rwandan refugee camp with the warning that the camps were becoming the base for "another genocide."

No one should take those words lightly. Alain Destexhe, secretary-general of Doctors Without Borders, writes in *Foreign Policy* magazine that the killing in Rwanda was one of only three instances of genocide in this century (the others, he says, were the massacre of Armenians in World War I and of Jews and other minorities in World War II).

Although ethnic differences in Rwanda are often hard to detect, they are real to Hutus and Tutsis. The killing that began with a vengeance [in Spring 1994] met the definition of genocide because, while the Hutu leaders had identified some Hutu dissidents to be murdered, they had targeted all Tutsis for death.

In the two months beginning in April, Hutu militias killed 500,000, about half the Tutsi population. The rest hid in the hills or escaped to other countries. Perversely, the Hutu massacres gave new life to the armed Tutsi opposition, which by summer was asserting control over the country. As their own control waned, Hutu leaders played on fears of Tutsi retaliation to lead the flight of refugees to places like Goma, Zaire.

There's a further perversity. Since summer, Hutu leaders who directed the spring massacres have controlled the camps. They use death threats to prevent fellow Hutus from returning to Rwanda. They run services ranging from camp security to food distribution. According to many experts, they are organizing for a bloody return.

RELIEF DILEMMA

Relief agencies therefore face a frightful dilemma: Whether to aid Hutu refugees when the aid becomes a means for extremist Hutus to increase their power, or to undercut the extremists even if doing so means depriving innocent refugees. Difficult though such decisions are, and grim though events in Rwanda may become again, the question arises why the United States should involve itself at all. Rwanda is a tiny country of little strategic significance compared, say, with Russia or Brazil.

The answer is that while many of us prefer that the international community take the initiative in such matters, no such "community" can function without the participation of the world's leading power. The community comes apart when the United States stands aside or, as in the case of Rwanda, pushes for nonintervention.

Two weeks after the spring slaughter erupted, the UN Security Council ordered the UN force in Rwanda cut from 2,500 to 270. Two weeks later the Administration published a Presidential decision directive on peacekeeping that did more than place severe limits on U.S. participation in such operations. Because of the need for U.S. support of UN operations, the directive effectively constrained even peacekeeping in which the United States is not involved.

Although the massacres continued, U.S. objections stalled the UN secretary-general's plea to return the peacekeepers with a stronger mandate and better equipment. This was not armchair strategy by distant bureaucrats. The Canadian general on the scene in Rwanda said he could have stopped the genocide with the mixed force he had before it was cut, or even with a few hundred paratroopers.

Until the killings subsided, U.S. and UN officials declined to call them genocide. No wonder. Had they done so, they would have been required by the UN Convention on Genocide to take the forceful actions they preferred to avoid. Still, even if the Clinton Administration wanted to, how could it act quickly to help quell upheavals like that in Rwanda, which erupted so suddenly? Holly Burkhalter, Washington director of Human Rights Watch, writes in *World Policy Journal* that the warnings had mounted for more than two years and had became acute in Spring 1994.

NATURAL DISASTER

Perhaps because crises like that of Rwanda are ugly, confusing and complex, the images that often stay with us are those of success in the aftermath: U.S. airlifts, public and private aid providers, survivors with rekindled hope.

However valid, such images distract attention from the need for crisis prevention. That was one of the themes running through a conference organized by the World Peace Foundation and Brown University's Institute for International Studies. John Hammock, president of Oxfam America and one of the conference participants, made the point well. In criticism that includes humanitarian organizations and media as well as policymakers, Hammock wrote:

"There is a strong tendency to view all emergencies as if they were the equivalent of a natural disaster, beyond the control of people and, thus, avoid a serious assessment of the factors which created the crisis."

The Clinton Administration has had time to assess the factors leading to the Rwandan crisis. One wonders whether it will apply that knowledge to preventing the next one.

INTERPRETING EDITORIAL CARTOONS

This activity may be used as an individualized study guide for students in libraries and resource centers or as a discussion catalyst in small group and classroom discussions.

Although cartoons are usually humorous, the main intent of most political cartoonists is not to entertain. Cartoons express serious social comment about important issues. Using graphics and visual arts, the cartoonist expresses opinions and attitudes. By employing an entertaining and often light-hearted visual format, cartoonists may have as much or more impact on national and world issues as editorial and syndicated columnists.

Points to Consider:

1. Examine the cartoon in Reading 24.

2. How would you describe the message of this cartoon? Try to describe the message in one to three sentences.

3. Do you agree with the message expressed in this cartoon? Why or why not?

4. Does the cartoon support the author's point of view in any of the readings in this book? If the answer is yes, be specific about which reading or readings and why.

5. Are any of the readings in Chapter Four in basic agreement with this cartoon?

BIBLIOGRAPHY

The Holocaust

Barnett, Victoria J., **For the Soul of the People,** New York: Oxford University Press, 1992.

Bauer, Yehuda, **The Holocaust in Historical Perspective,** Seattle: University of Washington Press, 1978.

Browning, Christopher, **Ordinary Men: Reserve Battalion 101 and the Final Solution in Poland,** New York: Harper Collins, 1992.

Dawidowicz, Lucy, **The Holocaust and the Historians,** Cambridge, MA: Harvard University Press, 1981.

Goldhagen, Daniel J., **Hitler's Willing Executioners: Ordinary Germans and the Holocaust,** New York: Alfred A. Knopf, 1996.

Langbein, Hermann, **Against All Hope: Resistance in the Nazi Concentration Camps, 1938-1945,** New York: Continuum, 1996.

Lipstadt, Deborah, **Denying the Holocaust: The Growing Assault on Truth and Memory,** New York: Free Press, 1993.

Kaplan, Marion A., **Between Dignity and Despair: Jewish Life in Nazi Germany,** New York: Oxford University Press, 1998.

Katz, Stephen T., **The Holocaust in Historical Context,** New York: Oxford University Press, 1994.

Rosenbaum, Alan S., **Is the Holocaust Unique? Perspectives in Comparative Genocide,** Boulder, Co: Westview Press, 1992.

The Americas

Axelrod, Alan, **Chronicle of the Indian Wars from Colonial Times to Wounded Knee,** New York: Prentice Hall, 1993.

de Las Casas, Bartolome, **Account of the First Voyages and Discoveries Made by the Spaniards in America,** London: J. Darby, 1699.

Chomsky, Noam, **Powers and Prospects: Reflections on Human Nature and the Social Order,** Boston: South End Press, 1996.

Crum, Stephen J., **The Road on Which We Came: A History of the Western Shoshone,** Salt Lake City: University of Utah Press, 1994.

Eckert, Allan W., **That Dark and Bloody River: Chronicles of the Ohio River Valley,** New York: Bantam, 1995.

Pettitpas, Katherine, **Severing the Ties that Bind: Government Repression of Indigenous Religious Ceremonies on the Prairies,** Winnipeg: University of Manitoba Press, 1994.

Schlessinger, Stephen C., **Bitter Fruit: The Untold Story of the American Coup in Guatemala,** Garden City, NY: Anchor Press, 1983.

Solnit, Rebecca, **Savage Dreams: A Journey into the Hidden Wars of the American West,** San Francisco: Sierra Club, 1998.

Stannard, David E., **American Holocaust: Columbus and the Conquest of the New World,** New York: W.W. Norton, 1994.

Zinn, Howard, **A People's History of the United States,** New York: Harper & Row, 1980.

Cambodia

Ashe, Var Hong, **From Phnom Phen to Paradiste: Escape from Cambodia,** London: Hodder and Stoughton, 1998.

Boua, Cahnthou, "Genocide of a Religious Group: Pol Pot and Cambodia's Buddhist Monks," in **State Organized Terror: The Case of Violent Internal Repression,** Schlapentokh, et al., eds., Boulder, CO: Westview Press, 1991.

Cambodian Culture Since 1975: Homeland and Exile, M. Ebihara et al., Ithaca: Cornell University Press, 1994.

Chandler, David P., **Brother Number One: A Political Biography of Pol Pot,** Boulder, CO: Westview Press, 1999.

Haas, Michael, **Cambodia, Pol Pot and the United States,** New York: Praeger, 1991.

Kiernan, Ben, **The Pol Pot Regime: Race, Power and Genocide Under the Khmer Rouge, 1975-1979,** New Haven: Yale University Press, 1996.

Ponchaud, Francois, **Cambodia Year Zero,** London: Allen Lane, 1978.

Revolution and Its Aftermath in Kampuchea: Eight Essays, David P. Chandler and Ben Kiernan, eds., New Haven: Yale University Press, 1983.

Stuart-Fox, Martin and Bunheang Ung, **The Murderous Revolution: Life and Death in Pol Pot's Kampuchea,** Sydney: APCOL, 1985.

The Third Indochina Conflict, David W.P. Elliot, ed., Boulder, CO: Westview Press, 1981.

Rwanda

Adleman, Howard and Astri Shurke, **The Path of Genocide: The Rwanda Crisis from Uganda to Zaire,** New Brunswick, NJ: Transnational Publishers, 1998.

Des Forges, Alison, **Leave None to Tell the Story: Genocide in Rwanda,** New York: Human Rights Watch, 1999.

Destexhe, Alain, **Rwanda and Genocide in the Twentieth Century,** New York: New York University Press, 1995.

Evans, Glynne, **Responding to the Crises in the African Great Lakes,** Oxford: Oxford University Press, 1997.

Gourevitch, Philip, **We Wish to Inform You that Tomorrow We Will Be Killed with Our Families: Stories from Rwanda,** New York: Farrar, Strauss, and Giroux, 1998.

Klinghoffer, Arthur Jay, **The International Dimension of Genocide in Rwanda,** New York: New York University Press, 1998.

Leyton, Elliot, **Touched by Fire: Doctors Without Borders in the Third World Crisis,** Toronto: M & S, 1998.

O'Halloran, Patrick J., **Humanitarian Intervention and Genocide in Rwanda,** London: Research Institute for the Study of Conflict and Terror, 1995.

Prunier, Gerard, **The Rwanda Crisis: History of Genocide,** New York: Columbia University Press, 1995.

Uvin, Peter, **Development, Aid and Conflict: Reflections from the Case of Rwanda,** Helsinki: UN World Institute for Development Economics Research, 1996.

General

Campbell, Greg, **The Road to Kosovo: A Balkan Diary,** Boulder, CO: Westview Press, 1999.

Dubkowski, Michael N. and Isador Williman, **The Coming of Age of Scarcity: Preventing Mass Death and Genocide in the 21st Century**, Syracuse: Syracuse University Press, 1998.

Fonseca, Isabel, **Bury Me Standing: The Gypsies and Their Journey,** New York: Alfred A. Knopf, 1995.

Hovannisian, Richard G., **Remembrance and Denial: The Cost of the Armenian Genocide,** Detroit: Wayne State University Press, 1998.

Hochschild, Adam, **King Leopold's Ghost: A Story of Greed, Terror and Heroism in Colonial Africa,** New York: Houghton Mifflin, 1998.

Jardin, Matthew, **East Timor: Genocide in Paradise,** New York: Odonian Press, 1995.

Kaplan, Robert, **Balkan Ghosts: A Journey through Balkan History,** New York: St. Martin's Press, 1993.

Lemkin, Raphael, **Axis Rule in Occupied Europe,** Washington, D.C.: Carnegie Endowment for International Peace, 1944.

Minow, Martha, **Between Vengeance and Forgiveness: Facing History after Genocide and Mass Violence,** Boston: Beacon Press, 1998.

INDEX